The Anglican Cycle of Prayer — 1994

*O bless this people, Lord, who seek their own face
under the mask and can hardly recognize it...
O bless this people that breaks its bond...
And with them, all the peoples of North and South,
of East and West,
who sweat blood and sufferings,
and see, in the midst of these millions of waves
and sea swell of the heads of my people and grant to them warm
hands that they may clasp
the earth in a girdle of brotherly hands,
beneath the rainbow of thy peace.*

(Leopold Sedar Senghor)

FOREWORD by the International Director of the Anglican Fellowship of Prayer

When we think of Jesus at prayer, we normally focus on his earthly ministry—his hard fasting in the desert, the long night hours on the Galilean hillside, the miraculous healings, and his agonized prayer in the Garden of Gethsemane. But Jesus' prayer has not been confined to those few years in Israel almost 2,000 years ago. Jesus promised that he would always be with us, and even today he continues to pray for the church (Hebrews 7:25). When we pray each day for our church around the world, we are joined with this ongoing prayer of Jesus. Our church is Jesus' church. Our ministry is Jesus' ministry. And our prayer must be linked with Jesus' prayer. The best evangelism strategies, social services, stewardship and educational programs will never fulfil the mission of the church unless the indwelling Spirit of God gives them life and power.

The Lord prayed that he might be in us just as he is in the Father. He promised power for the church's needs through the gift of the Holy Spirit. This is how the world will come to know the Father's love (John 17). We are ineffective in our own strength, and that is true all around the world!

We pray the Anglican Cycle because we belong to one another. The Anglican Communion is a worldwide family of churches, and as we pray for our family, a wonderful thing happens! We are joined together by the invisible ties of God's love. We may not be world travelers, but prayer unites us as nothing else can ever do. Barriers of language, race and culture fall away as we hold each other in prayer. And so we fulfil Jesus' earnest prayer "that they may all be one ..." It's a privilege each day to join in Jesus' ministry of prayer and action.

+Reginald Hollis

The Rt. Rev. Reginald Hollis

CONTENTS

The calendar is not intended to be followed rigidly. At any time, natural catastrophe or national crisis may make us want to pray for our brothers and sisters in other countries. You may also wish to write personally to those you remember in your prayers. If you do not know a bishop's address, it may usually be obtained through the provincial offices listed on pages 136-137.

The Church of Burundi, Rwanda, and Zaïre

1. **BOGA-ZAÏRE**
   • Bunia
2. **BUJUMBURA**
   • Bujumbura
3. **BUKAVU**
   • Bukavu
4. **BUTARE**
   • Butare
5. **BUYE**
   • Buye
6. **GITEGA**
   • Gitega
7. **KIGALI**
   • Kigali
8. **KISANGANI**
   • Kisangani
9. **SHYIRA**
   • Shyira
10. **SHABA**
    • Lubumbashi
11. **MATANA**
    • Matana
12. **BYUMUBA**
    • Byumba
13. **NORD-KIVU**
    • Butembo

LEGEND

———	Nation
·········	Diocese
●	See City

January 1 *(Holy Name) (Sudan Day)*.
  PRAY for the Sudan.

WEEK OF JANUARY 2   *2 Christmas*

PRAY for the Provinces of Burundi, Samuel Sindamuka, Primate, with its four dioceses; Rwanda, Augustin Nshamihigo, Archbishop, with its seven dioceses; and Zaire, P. Byankya Njojo, Archbishop, with its five dioceses.

In a geographical area of 2,399,172 square kilometres, and with a population of over 37,000,000, two percent of the people call themselves Anglicans, with 78 percent of the population identified as Christians. The three Provinces have three theological colleges and 15 Bible colleges. There are 440 clergy and 340 parishes striving to meet the needs of the people in these Francophone Provinces.

Burundi—PRAY for church planting in the towns of Karuzi, Ruyigi and Cankuzo which is part of our evangelization programme during this Decade of Evangelism. PRAY also for the new leaders elected democratically in 1993 so that they may be given wisdom for ruling the country in peace thus enabling the church to fulfil her ministry.

Rwanda—PRAY for this new Province.

Zaire—PRAY for the peace of the Lord in Zaire and for each of the dioceses; for the church's work of evangelism, medical and social work and development projects; and for the missionaries working in the Province of Zaire.

Monday: Bujumbura (Burundi), Pie Ntukamazina, Bishop.

  Buye (Burundi), Samuel Ndayisenga, Bishop.

  Gitega (Burundi), Jean Nduwayo, Bishop. PRAY for the new leaders of the country who were elected democratically so that they may be given wisdom in their leadership, thus allowing the church to express her faith freely; and for the provision of funds for church-planting in the towns of Karuzi, Ruyigi, Muyinga and around Gitega.

Tuesday: **Matana (Burundi),** Samuel Sindamuka, Bishop.

Butare (Rwanda), Justin Ndandali, Bishop.

Byumba (Rwanda), Onesphore Rwaje, Bishop. GIVE THANKS to God for strong Christian faith of displaced people living in desperate conditions in refugee camps. PRAY for training of catechists and pastors to carry on the work of evangelism; for God's guidance, strength and wisdom as we carry on ministry amongst displaced people; and for peace, justice and reconciliation in Rwanda.

Wednesday: **Cyangugu (Rwanda),** Daniel Nduhura, Bishop.

Kigali (Rwanda), Adoniya Sebununguri, Bishop.

Kigeme (Rwanda), Alexis Bilindabagabo, Bishop.

Thursday *(The Epiphany)*—**Shyira (Rwanda),** Augustin Nshamihigo, Bishop.

Shyogwe (Rwanda), Samuel Musabyimana, Bishop.

Boga-Zaire, P. Byankya Njojo, Bishop. PRAY for resolution of continuing difficulties in the country; for unity among the political authorities; and for a peaceful solution to the tribal war which is affecting two tribes of the diocese.

Friday: **Bukavu (Zaire),** Jean Balufuga Dirokpa, Bishop.

Kisangani (Zaire), Sylvestre Tibefa Mugera, Bishop.

Saturday: **Nord-Kivu (Zaire),** Methusela M. Munzenda, Bishop. PRAY for the political situation of our country and for its people suffering the effects of high inflation. PRAY for the Diocesan Programmes in Evangelism (through the Diocesan Missionary Association), training of ministers and development work; for its medical service and the Mothers' Union; and PRAY for the Bishop that God would guide him in his new role.

Shaba (Zaire), Emmanuel Kolini Mbona, Bishop.

PRAY for the Church of the Province of Central Africa, W. P. Khotso Makhulu, Archbishop, with its 10 dioceses.

Founded in 1955, this Province includes four countries, Botswana, Malawi, Zambia and Zimbabwe. It covers a total area of 718,940 square miles. Each of the countries forming the Province faces different problems which have challenged Anglicans to participate in solving them.

There are over 600,000 Anglicans out of a total population of 22,000,000, with 8,000,000 Christians. Almost 400 clergy serve people in 200 parishes.

THANK GOD for the gift of rain in the Province, ending a severe drought. PRAY for wisdom in the formation of the Religious Communities Advisory Council, and for an increase in vocations to the sacred ministry and religious life.

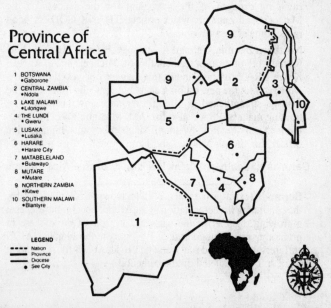

Province of Central Africa

1 BOTSWANA
• Gaborone
2 CENTRAL ZAMBIA
• Ndola
3 LAKE MALAWI
• Lilongwe
4 THE LUNDI
• Gweru
5 LUSAKA
• Lusaka
6 HARARE
• Harare City
7 MATABELELAND
• Bulawayo
8 MUTARE
• Mutare
9 NORTHERN ZAMBIA
• Kitwe
10 SOUTHERN MALAWI
• Blantyre

LEGEND
- - - Nation
⎯⎯ Province
⎯⎯ Diocese
• See City

Monday: Botswana, Archbishop W.P. Khotso Makhulu, Bishop.
Central Zambia, Clement W. Hlanya-Shaba, Bishop.

Tuesday: Harare (Zimbabwe), Peter R. Hatendi, Bishop.
Lake Malawi, Peter N. Nyanja, Bishop.

Wednesday: The Lundi (Zimbabwe), Jonathan Siyachitema, Bishop. GIVE THANKS for the cooperation of churches, state and people against the drought. PRAY for recovery from the effects of drought; for more clergy; and for our diocesan link with Southwark.
Lusaka (Zambia), Stephen Mumba, Bishop.

Thursday: Manicaland (Zimbabwe), Elijah M.P. Masuko, Bishop.
PRAY for Anglican missionaries throughout the world.

Friday: Matabeleland (Zimbabwe), Theophilus Tswere Naledi, Bishop. PRAY for good rains this year to recover from the ravaging drought of the past; and for the success of the Matabeleland Zambezi water project. THANK GOD for good rains in the season of 1992-93.
Northern Zambia, Bernard A. Malango, Bishop. THANK GOD for the work of the new Cathedral of St. Michael and All Angels, Kitwe. PRAY for the Canons, that they may be vessels of God's work; and for the new training chaplain, Fr. Colin Marsh, that he may be strengthened in his ministry, advising the Bishop on training matters. PRAY also for C.M. Mbambi, a VSO agriculturalist, and the Rev. William Muchombo, an administrative officer, for Chipili Mission and Farm Project.

Saturday: Southern Malawi, Nathaniel Benson Aipa, Bishop.

Bermuda (extra-provincial), William Down, Bishop. PRAY for the continuing implementation of the overall plan for the diocese; a growing together of the parishes; the role of the diocese in promoting racial integration; and ministry to the addicted, AIDS sufferers, tourists and seafarers. GIVE THANKS for restoration work so far completed on the cathedral.

Anglican Communion Sunday—GIVE THANKS for the witness of our brothers and sisters in the Anglican Communion throughout the world. PRAY for the Anglican Consultative Council and for the Secretary General, and for members of his staff.

O God, Giver of life and source of all wisdom, grant us Your power and might; shine in us Your bright Light; penetrate our hearts; and clean out all our doubts and emptiness. Enable us in this Decade of Evangelism to reach the unreached, to support the underprivileged, to shine as Your Light in the darkness and to encourage one another. Make each of us feel concern and challenge; send us out in Your power to do Your will.

The Church of Uganda

Monday: Bukedi, Nicodemus Okille, Bishop.

Bunyoro-Kitara, Wilson Nkuna Turumanya, Bishop. THANK GOD for the spirit of reconciliation and forgiveness in the diocese; and for brothers and sisters in the Lord abroad. PRAY that the Holy Spirit may convict many to be renewed during this Decade of Evangelism and renewal period.

Busoga, Cyprian Bamwoze, Bishop.

Tuesday *(Confession of St. Peter)* **Week of Prayer for Christian Unity Begins. PRAY for the World Council of Churches, Konrad Raizer, General Secretary, and for all councils of churches.**

East Ankole, Elisha Kyamugambi, Bishop. GIVE THANKS for the growth of the church in spite of present economic and ethical problems. PRAY for us as we endeavour to implement our plans to raise medical units, vocational schools for school drop-outs and other rural services; for the Diocesan Mission outreach; and for training of more personnel.

Kampala, Yona Okoth, Bishop.

PRAY for Roman Catholics.

Wednesday: Karamoja, Peter Lomongin, Bishop.

Kigezi, William Rukirande, Bishop. PRAY for training of the clergy, lay men and women and youths to reach out to evangelize and follow up; and for many people who are coming to the Lord as their personal Savior, that they will continue to grow. THANK GOD for the Cathedral under construction.

PRAY for Orthodox churches.

Thursday: Lango, Melchizedek Otim, Bishop.

Luwero, Mesusera Bugimbi, Bishop. PRAY for a steady growth in Christ; for the plan for outreach with the Gospel to all areas of the diocese, begun with all pastors training conference in June, 1993; and that the Holy Spirit will guide us.

PRAY for Lutherans.

Friday: Madi and West Nile, Caleb A.M. Nguma, Bishop. GIVE THANKS with all those who will celebrate the Diocesan Silver Jubilee on 28th January. PRAY for 200,000 Prayer/Hymn books in Lugbara. GIVE THANKS for the successful inauguration of the diocese of Nebbi.

PRAY for Methodists.

Mbale, Israel Wamambisi Koboyi, Bishop. PRAY for God's guidance for our Bishop; for co-operation of his senior staff; for God's Spirit to awaken the spirit of worship, Christian giving and evangelism; and for mending St. Andrew's Cathedral roof. THANK GOD for the freedom of worship and evangelism in Uganda.

Saturday: Mityana, Wilson Mutebi, Bishop. THANK GOD for meeting our daily financial needs; and for the vehicles he has given us. PRAY that the Decade of Evangelism may continue to bear lasting fruits; and for our Ten Year's Development Plan, that Christians may use it as a guideline for bringing about lasting and God-glorifying growth of our diocese.

Muhabura, Ernest M. Shalita, Bishop. THANK God for many blessings; and for various projects which are taking off, particularly in education and health. PRAY that we may find workers in health and vocational training; that the government will see the need to construct roads in the northern part of the diocese; and for the country in this year of general elections.

PRAY for Baptists.

The Church of Uganda

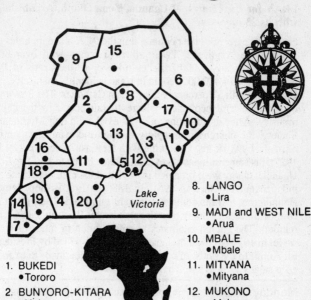

Lake Victoria

1. BUKEDI
   ● Tororo
2. BUNYORO-KITARA
   ● Hoima
3. BUSOGA
   ● Jinja
4. EAST ANKOLE
   ● Mbarara
5. KAMPALA
   ● Kampala
6. KARAMOJA
   ● Moroto
7. KIGEZI
   ● Kabale

8. LANGO
   ● Lira
9. MADI and WEST NILE
   ● Arua
10. MBALE
    ● Mbale
11. MITYANA
    ● Mityana
12. MUKONO
    ● Mukono
13. NAMIREMBE
    ● Kampala
14. NORTH KIGEZI
    ● Rukungiri
15. NORTHERN UGANDA
    ● Gulu
16. RUWENZORI
    ● Fort Portal
17. SOROTI
    ● Soroti
18. SOUTH RUWENZORI
    ● Kasese
19. WEST ANKOLE
    ● Bushenyi
20. WEST BUGANDA
    ● Masaka

LEGEND

▬ ▬ ▬ Nation
▬▬▬▬ Diocese
● See City

11

PRAY for the Church of Uganda, Yona Okoth, Archbishop, with its 23 dioceses.

Nearly 40 percent of the population in the 91,134 square miles of Uganda are Anglicans. Twenty-three dioceses with over 800 clergy and nearly 7,000 parishes minister to the needs of the people. Over 14,400,000 people in Uganda identify themselves as Christians with 38 percent being Roman Catholics. The Province maintains several theological colleges to train people for the active ministry. After its founding in 1877 by the Church Missionary Society, the church grew rapidly through the evangelisation of Africans by Africans. Beginning with the East Africa Revival in 1927, this same influence is evident in the church today. The first Ugandan clergy were ordained in 1893 and the church became an independent Province in 1961. In 1886 its first Bishop, James Hannington, and his companions were murdered. Their death is commemorated in many church calendars of the Anglican Communion. The church continues to suffer much in times of civil strife. In 1977 Archbishop Janani Luwum was killed by President Idi Amin. In the midst of conflict the church continues to experience steady growth and renewal.

Monday: Mukono, Livingstone Mpalanyi-Nkoyoyo, Bishop.

Namirembe, Misaeri Kauma, Bishop. THANK GOD for a new bishop as Bishop Kauma retires at the end of 1994; for those sick with AIDS; for deeper biblical understanding of death as the necessary door into eternal life; for a change to Christian sexual behavior; and for a general election due in 1994.

PRAY for Reformed, Congregational, and Presbyterian churches.

Tuesday*(Conversion of St. Paul)* **Week of Prayer for Christian Unity ends.**

Nebbi, Henry Orombi, Bishop.

North Kigezi, Yustasi Ruhindi, Bishop. THANK GOD for increasing peace and stability; for the strengthening of existing work; and for outreach programmes. PRAY for the mission to the

Pygmies; for ministry to those with AIDS and their orphans; and for grace and resources for these opportunities.

PRAY for Pentecostal churches.

Wednesday (*Australia Day*): **PRAY for Australia.**

Thursday: **Northern Uganda,** Gideon A. Oboma, Bishop.

Ruwenzori, Eustace Kamanyire, Bishop.

Soroti, Geresom Ilukor, Bishop. THANK GOD for his Providence, especially in enabling the completion of the Cathedral extension; and for increased peace and stability in the area. PRAY for funds for the Diocesan Five-Year Development Plan; and for the work of re-settling people displaced by insurgency.

South Rwenzori, Zebedee K. Masereka, Bishop. GIVE THANKS for ongoing successful Discipleship and Evangelism Training programs; that now all the parishes have vicars to take charge of them. PRAY for willingness among Christians to give of what God has given them to support the ever increasing ministry of the church.

West Ankole, Yoramu Bamunoba, Bishop.

West Buganda, Christopher D. Senyonjo, Bishop.

PRAY for Oriental Orthodox Christians.

Friday: **Tasmania** (extra-provincial to Australia), Phillip K. Newell, Bishop; Ronald F. Stone, Assistant. GIVE THANKS for the opportunities for mission and ministry in preaching, social concern, spiritual and pastoral care. PRAY for a new vision and initiatives in rural and urban ministries and stewardship development.

PRAY for Old Catholic Churches.

PRAY for the Church of Sweden.

Saturday: **Venezuela** (extra-provincial), Onell A. Soto, Bishop. PRAY for resources, human and material, needed for our transition from a chaplaincy church to a missionary national church; for strengthening of existing work; for missionary outreach; and for new ordinands. Map, p. 100.

PRAY for martyrs and prisoners of conscience.

PRAY for the province of Armagh, Ireland, Robert H.A. Eames, Primate of All Ireland and Archbishop of Armagh, with its seven dioceses.

The Church of Ireland, encompassing the two jurisdictions of Ireland, faces a period of national change. Political developments, opposition to paramilitary violence and the changing social picture of Ireland present challenges for all the churches in Ireland. Secularism has become a new ingredient for a largely traditional and conservative country. In Northern Ireland sectarianism makes support for violence possible.

PRAY for the Archbishop of Armagh as he seeks to give Christian leadership in the tensions of Northern Ireland and its border areas; for the work of the Church of Ireland in bringing about reconciliation of the different traditions, separated for generations by political and religious identities; and for the pastoral care of people who face vast changes to their life-style in urban and rural areas.

Map, p. 50.

Monday: Armagh, Archbishop Robert H.A. Eames, Bishop. PRAY for work of reconciliation in a divided community; for those who suffer because of violence; for spiritual renewal in the church in Ireland; and for greater understanding among the people of different traditions.

Clogher, Brian Hannon, Bishop. PRAY for steady parish leadership in building trust and dialogue at every level in church and state in our cross-border diocese. GIVE THANKS for the sense of teamwork and mutual responsibility among our varied family of diocesan clergy and their spouses.

Tuesday: Connor, Samuel Poyntz, Bishop. GIVE THANKS for the blessings from the 1993 Diocesan Week of Mission. Remember the International Year of the Family 1994 and PRAY that God's plan of family life may be accepted everywhere; for clerical family life; for broken homes; and for a return to Christian standards of faithfulness in marriage.

Derry and Raphoe, James Mehaffey, Bishop. GIVE THANKS for the solid foundations being laid through the development of the Vision 2000 diocesan programme with its objective of a renewed church reaching out into the community. PRAY for new partnerships in ministry between clergy and laity based on mutual respect and trust.

Wednesday *(The Presentation)*—**Down and Dromore,** Gordon McMullan, Bishop. GIVE THANKS for the support, ministry and dedication of clergy families and for those lay persons who serve so faithfully as organists and choirmembers.

Kilmore, Elphin and Ardagh, William Gilbert Wilson, Bishop.

Thursday: Tuam, Killala and Achonry, John Neill, Bishop. PRAY that more clergy may offer themselves for ministry in isolated areas; that there may be a growing sense of Christian stewardship in local congregations; and that a way may be found to address pressing financial needs. GIVE THANKS for the growth in lay ministry, and for the faithful service of the small team of priests in this diocese.

––––––––––

Cuba (extra-provincial), David Alvarez, Interim Bishop. Map p. 100.

Friday: PRAY for the Polish National Catholic Church and other Old Catholic Churches.

Saturday: PRAY for lay ministries.

Father, I am a man of my time and situation. Around me, the signs and symbols of man's fear, hatred, alienation;... It's not that we haven't tried, Father, to find ways to peace and reconciliation but always too little, too late; the forces of opposition were too great. My hopes have been destroyed. But the death of things I hoped for has been celebrated by others as victory in your power, Father... I am perplexed, angry, hopeless, sick, I want to turn my back, wash my hands, save myself, my family, get out. But every time I turn to go, there stands in my way a cross... Lord, make me a child of hope, reborn from apathy, cynicism, and despair... I do have hope grounded on your victory over power of evil, death itself; focused on your kingdom... And I do see signs of hope immediately around me... I see a sign—flowers growing on a bombed-out site. The sign—an empty cross. The burden, Lord, is yours. Lord I am a prisoner of hope! There is a life before death.

(A Prayer from Northern Ireland)

15

The Anglican Church in Aotearoa, New Zealand, and Polynesia

1. AUCKLAND
   • Auckland
2. CHRISTCHURCH
   • Christchurch
3. DUNEDIN
   • Dunedin
4. BISHOPRIC OF AOTEAROA
   • Regions A, B, C, D
5. NELSON
   • Nelson
6. POLYNESIA
   • Suva, Fiji Islands
7. WAIAPU
   • Napier, Hawkes Bay
8. WAIKATO
   • Hamilton
9. WELLINGTON
   • Wellington

SAMOA

TONGA

FIJI ISLANDS

LEGEND
— Diocese
• See City

(New Zealand Day) **PRAY for the Anglican Church of Aotearoa, New Zealand and Polynesia, Brian Davis, Archbishop, with its eight dioceses.**

The Anglican Church in Aotearoa, New Zealand and Polynesia is now a church of three partners, bound together in a new covenant relationship in the terms of a completely revised constitution, which expresses and entrenches an equality of partnership as between three distinct cultural groupings. This has enabled it to put its own house in order, so that during this Decade of Evangelism it is able with a clear conscience to invite others into that house, and to make them feel comfortable. The three partners are made up of the seven New Zealand dioceses, of Polynesia, and Te Pihopatanga o Aotearoa.

> *God of our nation*
> *you have called us to care for one another;*
> *cleanse our eyes to see each other clearly;*
> *open our hearts to know our own mistakes;*
> *build in us respect for each other's taonga;*
> *help us to do one another justice,*
> *and to hope together.*
> *God of covenant and calling,*
> *you bind us together;*
> *keep us faithful to our calling*
> *and true to our promises.*

PRAY for New Zealand.

Monday: Auckland (New Zealand), Bruce C. Gilberd, Bishop; Bruce McG. Moore, Regional Bishop. GIVE THANKS for the constitution which gives recognition to the three partners within the church: European, Maori and Pacific Islanders. PRAY for the success of the Decade of Evangelism; for the ministry of Holy Trinity Cathedral; and for the completion of the building programme.

Christchurch (New Zealand), David Coles, Bishop. PRAY for Anglican Social Services as they face growing demands following government welfare cuts. GIVE THANKS for developing strategies for mission and evangelism in the parishes.

Tuesday: Dunedin (New Zealand), Penelope A.B. Jamieson, Bishop. PRAY for the growth of local ministry and mission; for our rural parishes engaged in the Total Ministry Programme; for the Christian engagement of both lay and ordained with unjust structures and situations in our country; and for the guidance of Christ in all we do.

PRAY for Whakahuihui Vercoe, Bishop of Aotearoa.

Wednesday: Nelson (New Zealand), Derek Eaton, Bishop. GIVE THANKS for significant growth in the diocese, and continue to PRAY for effective evangelism and church planting.

Polynesia, Jabez L. Bryce, Bishop. PRAY for the Archdeaconry Councils and decentralization of administration; for outreach to the Chinese population; for Fiji as it returns to parliamentary government; and for effective Ministry Training in ethnic groupings in Fijian, Tongan, Samoan, English and Hindi.

Thursday: Waiapu (New Zealand), Murray John Mills, Diocesan Bishop serving the Hawke's Bay and Eastland regions; George H.D. Connor, Bishop in the Bay of Plenty. GIVE THANKS and PRAY for new expressions of rural, lay and youth ministry; for evangelistic outreach through developing relationships with two pihopatanga and between regions and parishes.

Friday: Waikato (New Zealand), David John Moxon, Bishop. THANK GOD for the ministry of our new Bishop; and for the gift of the gospel of Jesus Christ. PRAY that the diocese may focus on training and enabling all the baptized to live out and tell the Good News with enthusiasm; and that our partnership with Maori and Polynesian sectors help model a community of grace.

Saturday: Wellington (New Zealand), Archbishop Brian Davis, Bishop; Muru Walters, Assistant. PRAY for a continuing commitment to the Decade of Evangelism; for a restoration of an effective Catechumenate; and for the creative development of cultural partnership.

Costa Rica (Iglesia Episcopal Costarricense—extra provincial), Cornelius J. Wilson, Bishop.

PRAY for the Holy Catholic Church in Japan (Nippon Sei Ko Kai), Christopher I. Kikawada, Primate, with its 11 dioceses.

The Japanese society in general seems to have enjoyed a relatively stable and peaceful life through its economical prosperity during the past decade or so. But in reality, both the state and the people have failed to resolve accumulated social problems: immoral political practices, historical guilt of the past war and colonization, a whole range of environmental issues, exploitation of increasing numbers of migrant workers, ambiguous direction of Japan's international political roles, and various levels of human rights issues.

Nippon Sei Ko Kai is facing two-fold challenges, one in the society and another for itself: how NSKK can be a faithful witnessing community as a minority church in the midst of a secular and yet multi-religious society and how NSKK is able to strengthen and to increase its members (congregations, laity and clergy), which is apparently aging very fast demographically in coming years.

GIVE THANKS that the Community of Nazareth has been given a new site and facility for their religious life. PRAY for the increase of those called to the ordained ministry, as the present clergy are aging fast and there will soon be a shortage; for more mature and renewing faith of the people so that the whole church may find ways together in the debate on the ordination of women.

Monday: Chubu, Samuel W. Hoyo, Bishop. PRAY for increase of candidates for ordination; for a plan for developing local house churches; and for a mission plan based on the Bishop's pastoral letter.

Hokkaido, Augustine H. Amgai, Bishop. PRAY for the 24 churches of the diocese; for 9 welfare institutions; for Tomakomai Missions to Seamen; for international youth dormitory development in Sapporo; for increase of clergy; and for restoration of the native human rights of the Ainu People.

Tuesday: Kita Kanto, James T. Yashiro, Bishop. PRAY for an increase of candidates for ordination; and for success of the continuing education course for clergy. GIVE THANKS for continuing companionship with Dhaka, Bangladesh, and Central Pennsylvania, USA.

Kobe, John J. Furumoto, Bishop. PRAY for all 28 churches that they may be like the early church—faithful to the mission given from Christ, prayerful in one mind, hearing the Word of God together, a loving and forgiving body amazing in the eyes of all people, serving those from outside who come in open love; for new mission stations in Kurashiki and northwest Kobe; for the plan for the new diocesan office building; for those candidates studying in seminary—H. Kawamura, T. Takeuchi, and I. Hirano.

Ash Wednesday: **Kyoto,** John T. Okano, Bishop. PRAY for spiritual development of all laity and clergy; for lively mission action according to God's will; for increase of assistance to people in local society and the world; and to strengthen the work of educational and welfare institutions to the Glory of God.

Kyushu, Joseph N. Iida, Bishop. PRAY for the ability to work together for God's mission. GIVE THANKS for beginning of the program for training in joint clergy/laity ministry.

Thursday: Okinawa, Paul S. Nakamura, Bishop. PRAY for the increase of candidates for ordination and for the increase of lay readers in the diocese. GIVE THANKS for "Okinawa Diocese Day—March 21," the 43rd Anniversary of the arrival of two American missionaries to Okinawa; and for the consecration on Okinawa Diocese Day, 1993, of the Diocesan Columbarium, a sign of the indigenization of the Faith in Okinawa.

Osaka, Christopher I. Kikawada, Bishop and Primate. PRAY for the Sei Ko Kai Ikuno Center in its work of enabling Koreans and other non-Japanese to live together with Japanese in harmony.

Friday: Tohoku, William T. Murakami, Bishop. PRAY for widespread renewal of fundamental faith to fulfill God's mission; for total ministry training; and for establishment of a financial base for diocesan projects.

Tokyo, John M. Takeda, Bishop. PRAY for clergy and laity working together, recognizing each person's God-given abilities, in support of a mission body open to caring for each other; and for continuing discussion, in trust and respect, of the ordination of women. GIVE THANKS for the continuing companionship at the grass roots level with the Diocese of Maryland, USA.

Saturday: Yokohama, Raphael S. Kajiwara, Bishop. PRAY for 31 churches and 4 mission points; for our renewal in "one mission" and in pastoral and evangelical activities. GIVE THANKS for the birth and consecration of St. Christopher's Church, Yokohama; for our partnership with Leicester, England; and for the Mission to Seamen.

PRAY for Buddhists in Japan and throughout the world.

The Nippon Sei ko kai
(Holy Catholic Church in Japan)

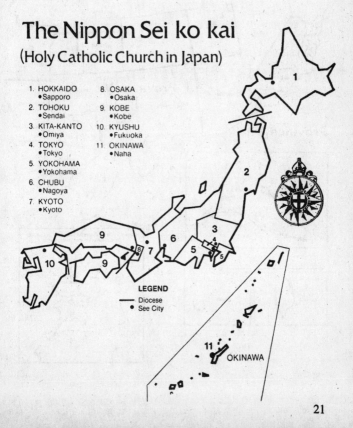

1. HOKKAIDO
   • Sapporo
2. TOHOKU
   • Sendai
3. KITA-KANTO
   • Omiya
4. TOKYO
   • Tokyo
5. YOKOHAMA
   • Yokohama
6. CHUBU
   • Nagoya
7. KYOTO
   • Kyoto
8. OSAKA
   • Osaka
9. KOBE
   • Kobe
10. KYUSHU
    • Fukuoka
11. OKINAWA
    • Naha

LEGEND
— Diocese
• See City

OKINAWA

21

The Episcopal

OLYMPIA · SPOKANE · MONTANA · NORTH DAKOTA · MINNESOTA

OREGON · EASTERN OREGON · IDAHO · SOUTH DAKOTA · IOWA

Province VI

WYOMING

NORTHERN CALIFORNIA · NEVADA · UTAH · COLORADO · NEBRASKA · WESTERN KANSAS · KANSAS · WEST MISSOURI

CALIFORNIA · EL CAMINO REAL · SAN JOAQUIN · LOS ANGELES · SAN DIEGO · ARIZONA · NAVAJOLAND · RIO GRANDE · NORTHWEST TEXAS · FORT WORTH · DALLAS · OKLAHOMA · ARKANSAS · WESTERN LOUISIANA

Province VII

TEXAS · WEST TEXAS

Province VIII

ALASKA

TAIWAN · HAWAII

CONVOCATION OF AMERICAN CHURCHES IN EUROPE
Under jurisdiction of the Presiding Bishop

Brussels · Frankfurt Wiesbaden · Paris · Munich · Geneva · Florence Rome

22

Church, USA

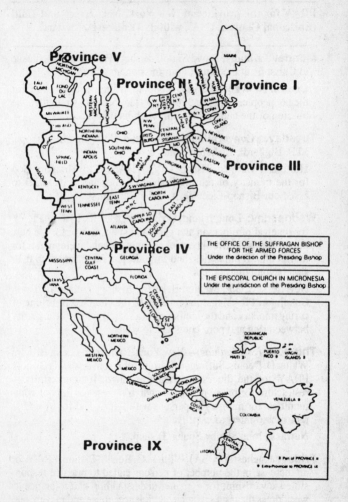

Province V

Province IV

Province I

Province III

Province IV

THE OFFICE OF THE SUFFRAGAN BISHOP
FOR THE ARMED FORCES
Under the direction of the Presiding Bishop

THE EPISCOPAL CHURCH IN MICRONESIA
Under the jurisdiction of the Presiding Bishop

Province IX

PRAY for the province of New York, New Jersey and Haiti (Episcopal Church, USA), with its 11 dioceses. (province II)

Monday: Albany, David S. Ball, Bishop. PRAY that obedience to Christ be at the heart of our mission and ministry.

Central New York (USA), David B. Joslin, Bishop. PRAY for the lay people, clergy and bishop as they work to strengthen the mission of the church in and through its parishes.

Tuesday: Convocation of American Churches in Europe, M.P. Bigliardi, Bishop-in-Charge.

Haiti, Luc Garnier, Bishop. GIVE THANKS to Almighty God for the ministry of retiring Bishop Garnier and ASK GOD to assist our Bishop-Elect, Jean Zaché Duracin.

Wednesday: Long Island, Orris G. Walker, Jr., Bishop. PRAY for renewal of diocesan and parochial stewardship; for the new nursing home in Brooklyn; for congregational development; for multi-cultural ministries; and for a deeper commitment to mission beyond our borders.

New Jersey, G.P. Mellick Belshaw, Bishop; Joe Morris Doss, Coadjutor. PRAY that the mission of the church will be one of caring ministry and reconciliation in a society where the disparity between rich and poor continues to widen.

Thursday (*St. Matthias*)—**New York,** Richard F. Grein, Bishop; Walter D. Dennis, Suffragan; Harold Robinson, Assisting Bishop. PRAY for the diocesan capital campaign; for our efforts to restructure for mission; for the church's presence in poor communities; for ministry to persons with AIDS; and for an end to racism and intergroup strife.

Newark, John Shelby Spong, Bishop.

Friday: Rochester (USA), William G. Burrill, Bishop. PRAY for an increase in the number of persons called to practice responsible stewardship; for a greater understanding and tolerance as we address the issues of societal violence, abuse and racism; and for a growing witness to the inclusiveness of the Gospel.

The Virgin Islands, Egbert Don Taylor, Bishop.

Saturday: Western New York, David C. Bowman, Bishop. PRAY for the work of our Urban Congregations as they attempt to meet the needs of the communities around them; and for our ministry to the aged through The Episcopal Church Home.

Puerto Rico (Iglesia Episcopal Puetorriquena)-(extra-provincial), David A. Alvarez, Bishop. PRAY for the ministry of our Bishop and the ministry of all priests, deacons and lay ministers; for our parochial and social ministries; and for the guidance of the Holy Spirit in our work and witness. Map p. 100.

Lord, when did we see you?

I was hungry and starving
    and you were obese;
Thirsty
    and you were watering your garden;
With no road to follow, and without hope
    and you called the police and were
    happy that they took me prisoner;
Barefoot and with ragged clothing
    and you were saying "I have nothing
    to wear, tomorrow I will buy something new"
Sick
    and you asked: "Is it infectious?"
Prisoner
    and you said: "That is where all those
    of your class should be"
Lord, have mercy!

PRAY for the Church of North India, John E. Ghose, Moderator, with its 23 dioceses.

The Church of North India was inaugurated in 1970 and is the union of six churches: The Anglican Church, the United Church of Northern India (Congregationalist and Presbyterian), the Methodist Church (British and Australian Conferences), the Council of Baptist Churches in Northern India, the Church of the Brethren in India, and the Disciples of Christ.

Map, p. 60.

Monday: Agra, Morris Andrews, Bishop.

Amritsar, Anand chandu Lal, Bishop.

Andaman and Nicobar, Edmund Matthew, Bishop.

Assam, Ernest W. Talibuddin, Bishop.

Tuesday *(St. David)* **PRAY for Wales**

Barrackpore, Brojen Malakar, Bishop.

Bhopal, Manohar B. Singh, Bishop.

Bombay, Samuel B. Joshua, Bishop.

Calcutta, Dinesh C. Gorai, Bishop.

Wednesday: Chandigarh, Joel Vidyasagal Mal, Bishop.

Chota Nagpur, Z. James Terom, Bishop.

Cuttack, D.K. Mohanty, Bishop.

Darjeeling, Bishop to to chosen. PRAY for unity in our faith and love and evangelisation and growth in spiritual strength and understanding of the true meaning of Christ's love for his children everywhere.

Thursday: Delhi, Pritam B. Santram, Bishop.

Durgapur, John E. Ghose, Acting Bishop.

Gujarat, Paul R. Chauhan, Bishop.

Jabalpur, Franklin C. Jonathan, Deputy Moderator.

Friday: Kolhapur, MacDonald Claudius, Bishop.

Lucknow, Arthur Raja Yusef, Bishop.

Nagpur, Vinod Peter, Bishop.

Nasik, Dinkar J. Vairagar, Bishop.

Saturday: North East India, Ernest W. Talibuddin, Bishop. GIVE THANKS for encouraging support of the pastorates for the Diocesan Central Fund. PRAY for the diocesan efforts through various programmes and projects for Leadership Development; and for Spiritual Renewal: Life and Mission of the Church.

Patna, N.M. Bagh, Bishop. PRAY for our pastorates, hospitals, schools, development and evangelistic ministries; and for dynamic leadership, youth and newly baptized Christians of Malto origin. GIVE THANKS for pastors and all dedicated workers of the church.

Rajasthan, E.C. Anthony, Bishop.

Sambalpur, Lingaram Tandy, Bishop.

Good Jesus, Fountain of Love,
Fill us with thy love.
Absorb us into thy love;
Compass us with thy love,
That we may see all things in the light of thy love,
Receive all things as the token of thy love,
Speak of all things in words breathing of thy love,
Win through thy love others to thy love,
Be kindled day by day with a new glow of thy love,
Until we be fitted to enter into thine everlasting love,
To adore thy love and love to adore thee, our God our all.
Even so come, O Lord Jesus.

(Edward Bouverie Pusey)

Anglican
Church of
Australia

PROVINCE OF NEW SOUTH WALES

1. SYDNEY
   • Sydney
2. ARMIDALE
   • Armidale
3. BATHURST
   • Bathurst
4. CANBERRA & GOULBURN
   • Goulburn
5. GRAFTON
   • Grafton
6. NEWCASTLE
   • Newcastle
7. RIVERINA
   • Narrandera

PROVINCE OF QUEENSLAND

8. BRISBANE
   • Bribane
9. CARPENTARIA
   • Thursday Island
10. N. QUEENSLAND
    • Townsville
11. NORTHERN TERRITORY
    • Darwin
12. ROCKHAMPTON
    • Rockhampton

LEGEND

----- Province
——— Diocese
• See City

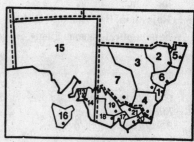

PROVINCE OF SOUTH AUSTRALIA

13. ADELAIDE
    • Adelaide
14. THE MURRAY
    • Murray Bridge
15. WILLOCHRA
    • Gladstone

PROVINCE OF VICTORIA

17. MELBOURNE
    • Melbourne
18. BALLARAT
    • Ballarat
19. BENDIGO
    • Bendigo
20. GIPPSLAND
    • Sale
21. WANGARATTA
    • Wangaratta

PROVINCE OF WESTERN AUSTRALIA

22. PERTH
    • Perth
23. BUNBURY
    • Bunbury
24. NORTHWEST AUSTRALIA
    • Geraldton

EXTRA PROVINCIAL*
16. TASMANIA
    • Hobart

PRAY for the province of South Australia, one of five provinces of the Anglican Church of Australia, Keith Rayner, Primate, Ian G.C. George, Archbishop, with its three dioceses.

Australia has been experiencng a period of great social change; unemployent is high, especially among young people; industry is being re-structured; governments have been cutting back programmes. There is a growing pressure for Australia to become a republic as a symbol of our independence and our membership of the Pacific and Asian regions. The Anglican Church is needing to show that it is not tied to the colonial past.

As society becomes steadily more mixed culturally the need for genuine ecumenism becomes stronger. Most of the world's Christian churches are represented here, and also the non-Christian faiths, and mutual understanding and action becomes increasingly important in a context of strong secularism and materialism.

The Anglican Church in Australia is still grappling with the aftermath of the decision to ordain women as priests. Dioceses, parishes and individuals opposed to the decision are questioning the implications of the resulting impairment of their communion with the rest of the church. Where women's priesthood has been accepted there is a growing appreciation of the new perspective on ministry that is developing.

Emphasis on the indigenous peoples of the world has helped white Australians to know better the culture of our Aboriginal brothers and sisters. The formation by the General Synod of a National Anglican Aboriginal Council has given a new impetus to the life of the Anglican Church among the descendants of the original inhabitants of our country
GIVE THANKS for the unifying force of the General Synod and for the work of its commissions, boards and committees. PRAY for justice and recognition for Aboriginal people; for healing of divisions within the church resulting from the priesting of women; and for effective evangelism among the unchurched.

Monday: Adelaide, Archbishop Ian George, Bishop. Stuart Smith, Assistant Bishop. PRAY for continued development of evangelism, welfare and justice initiatives; of the Aboriginal

Anglican Community; of new work in expanding suburbs; and for the unity of the diocese as we begin the ordination of women as priests.

Tuesday: **The Murray,** Graham H. Walden, Bishop.

Wednesday: Willochra, David McCall, Bishop. GIVE THANKS for the commitment of people and parishes in a time of rural recession. PRAY for those parishes and communities experiencing a decline in population and in community services.

Thursday: **The Lusitanian Church (Episcopal Church in Portugal),** Fernando Soares, Bishop.

Friday: Spanish Reformed Episcopal Church, Arturo Sanchez, Bishop. PRAY for a strong witness by this small church; for its missionary development; for the implementation of new churches; and for the success of the Decade of Evangelism.

Saturday: PRAY for the Church in China. The Chinese church is described as "post denominational," as most of the Protestant Churches, including the Anglican Church, came together to form the China Christian Council. The church is estimated to have 3,544,000 members.

May we who share Christ's body
live his risen life:
we who drink his cup
bring life to others;
we whom the Spirit lights
give light to the world.

(USPG Prayer)

PRAY for the province of Canada (one of four provinces of the Anglican Church of Canada), S. Stewart Payne, Metropolitan; with its seven dioceses.

Monday: **Central Newfoundland,** Edward Marsh, Bishop. PRAY for fishing communities facing problems arising from a moratorium in cod fishery; and that an effective religious education program may be continued and promoted in our provincial schools. THANK GOD for an increasing number of lay persons exercising their baptismal ministry.

Tuesday: **Eastern Newfoundland and Labrador,** Donald Harvey, Bishop. PRAY for Children and Youth Ministries; for ministry in a time of crisis in the fishery; and for ministry in a time of general economic instability and high unemployment.

Wednesday: **Fredericton,** George Lemmon, Bishop; Harold Nutter, Bishop Emeritus. PRAY for increased commitment to evangelism and stewardship; for inner-city ministries; for unity in pursuit of diocesan objectives; for lay ministry; for plans for our Sesquicentennial in 1995; continued strength of our companion relationship with Eldoret; and growth in understanding of ministry.

Thursday *(St. Patrick)*—**PRAY for Ireland.**

Montreal, Andrew S. Hutchison, Bishop. PRAY for the newly established Laos Institute (an institute for lay ministry) and for new initiatives in visioning; for growth in ministry with a French-speaking population; and for courage and imagination in the work of congregational development and evangelism.

Friday: **Nova Scotia,** Arthur G. Peters, Bishop; James Allan, Assistant Bishop. PRAY for a greater awareness and development of our understanding of total ministry as the Whole People of God in ministry and mission.

Saturday *(St. Joseph)*—**Quebec,** Bruce Stavert, Bishop. GIVE THANKS for the faithfulness of lay leaders in the many small congregations of the diocese; and for the lay readers. PRAY for guidance as the diocese and parishes face critical decisions in the face of reduced numbers and financial strains.

Western Newfoundland, Archbishop S. Stewart Payne, Bishop. PRAY for our fishermen, fish plant workers and the unemployed; for people involved in stewardship, renewal, Christian education, and youth work; and for more vocations to ministry, especially the ordained ministry. THANK GOD for his love and goodness.

O Jesus, poor and abject, unknown and despised, have mercy upon me and let me not be ashamed to follow you.

O Jesus, hated, calumniated, and persecuted, have mercy upon me, and let me not be afraid to come after you.

O Jesus, betrayed and sold at a vile price, have mercy upon me and make me content to be as my Master.

O Jesus, blasphemed, accused, and wrongfully condemned, have mercy upon me and teach me to endure the contradiction of sinners.

O Jesus, clothed with a habit of reproach and shame, have mercy upon me, and let me not seek my own glory.

O Jesus, insulted, mocked, and spit upon, have mercy upon me and let me run with patience the race set before me.

O Jesus, dragged to the pillar, scourged and bathed in blood, have mercy upon me, and let me not faint in the fiery trial.

O Jesus, crowned with thorns and hailed in derision;

O Jesus, burdened with our sins and the curses of the people;

O Jesus, affronted, outraged, buffeted, overwhelmed with injuries, griefs, and humiliations;

O Jesus, hanging on the accursed Tree, bowing the head, giving up the ghost, have mercy upon me, and conform my whole soul to your holy, humble, suffering Spirit.

(John Wesley)

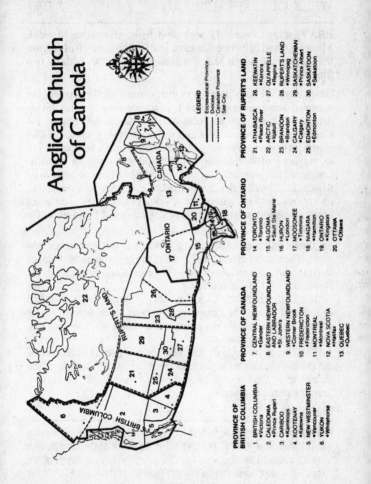

Anglican Church of Canada

LEGEND
- —— Ecclesiastical Province
- ------ Diocese
- ------ Canadian Province
- • See City

PROVINCE OF BRITISH COLUMBIA
1. BRITISH COLUMBIA
   • Victoria
2. CALEDONIA
   • Prince Rupert
3. CARIBOO
   • Kamloops
4. KOOTENAY
   • Kelowna
5. NEW WESTMINSTER
   • Vancouver
6. YUKON
   • Whitehorse

PROVINCE OF CANADA
7. CENTRAL NEWFOUNDLAND
   • Gander
8. EASTERN NEWFOUNDLAND AND LABRADOR
   • St. John's
9. WESTERN NEWFOUNDLAND
   • Corner Brook
10. FREDERICTON
    • Fredericton
11. MONTREAL
    • Montreal
12. NOVA SCOTIA
    • Halifax
13. QUEBEC
    • Quebec

PROVINCE OF ONTARIO
14. TORONTO
    • Toronto
15. ALGOMA
    • Sault Ste Marie
16. HURON
    • London
17. MOOSONEE
    • Timmins
18. NIAGARA
    • Hamilton
19. ONTARIO
    • Kingston
20. OTTAWA
    • Ottawa

PROVINCE OF RUPERT'S LAND
21. ATHABASCA
    • Peace River
22. ARCTIC
    • Iqaluit
23. BRANDON
    • Brandon
24. CALGARY
    • Calgary
25. EDMONTON
    • Edmonton
26. KEEWATIN
    • Kenora
27. QU'APPELLE
    • Regina
28. RUPERT'S LAND
    • Winnipeg
29. SASKATCHEWAN
    • Prince Albert
30. SASKATOON
    • Saskatoon

PRAY for the Church of Bangladesh, Bishop Barnabas Mondal, Moderator, with its two dioceses, and for the Church of Ceylon (Sri Lanka),Kenneth M.J. Fernando, Moderator, with its two dioceses.

Bangladesh is a Muslim country though not a Muslim state in the accepted sense, as is Pakistan. It is a poor country often hit by natural disasters such as flood and cyclone. In this context the Church of Bangladesh lives and works. It is very small (12,000 members in a country of over 120 million people), and carries out its ministry of development, relief and education in a multi-communal environment, working with Muslims, Hindus and Christians alike. The church is committed to leadership development in its various units and carries out training programmes at different levels, including a bachelor of theology course by extension for church workers and others.

Sri Lanka has been experiencing a civil war during the last few years. The war is between the forces of the government and that of the militants. The militants are fighting for a separate state in the North and East of the country.

It is in the midst of this reality that the church has been called to live and work. The Christians are about seven percent of the population. The Anglicans in the two dioceses are less than one percent of the population.

The church has to learn to accept the reality of the presence of the Buddhists, Hindus and the followers of Islam. The role of the church in this context is to work with others in the country to promote peace and justice.

Map, p.60.

Monday: Dhaka (Bangladesh), Barnabas Dwijen Mondal, Bishop and Moderator. GIVE THANKS for the work of the church as a small united church; and for the fellowship and support we receive from churches worldwide in times of disaster. PRAY for the further development of the church; for the theological lecturers and students, and all mission partners; for wisdom as the church moves to implement its decision to ordain women; and for growth in the bond of faith and love.

Tuesday: **Kushtia (Bangladesh),** Michael S. Baroi, Bishop.

Wednesday: **PRAY for the people of Islam.**

Thursday: **Colombo (Sri Lanka),** Kenneth Michael James Fernando, Bishop. PRAY for our new Bishop, for all our clergy and people, that God may use the new leadership in our midst to work amongst the victims of the war, the refugees, and all those suffering in so many ways, bringing about healing in the midst of brokenness.

Friday *(The Annunciation)*—**Kurunagala (Sri Lanka),** Andrew Kumarage, Bishop. PRAY for God's guidance and blessing as the diocese plans and implements a programme of work for the next few years with special emphasis on developing lay leadership and lay participation.

Saturday: **PRAY for Hindus.**

Come, Lord, and cover me with the night.
Spread your grace over us as you assured us you would do.
Your promises are more than all the stars in the sky;
Your mercy is deeper than the night.
Lord, it will be cold.
The night comes with its breath of death.
Night comes, the end comes,
but Jesus Christ comes also.
Lord, we wait for him day and night.

(A Prayer from West Africa)

PRAY for the Episcopal Church of Jerusalem and the Middle East, Samir Kafity, President-Bishop, with its four dioceses.

Dominating our concerns at this writing is the plight of 400 Palestinian deportees living in tents on a barren mountainside in South Lebanon. Pray for a resolution of this problem and the larger situation of the Arab-Israeli crisis. Pray for the people of the occupied territories and for those working for peace, among them Hanna Sharawi, a member of our church and a leader of the Palestinian peace delegation.

Thousands of displaced Sudanese places demands upon the resources of churches in Egypt and Jordan. Our principal ministry is to provide them with a sense of a "home from home"; many of them have been cut off from families for years.

The church in Iran continues to witness bravely to the gospel. The churches of the Gulf continue their ministry under stresses caused by uncertain politics associated with Iraq and Iran. They minister to thousands of ex-patriate Indian and Sri Lankan workers. Our church in Ethiopia provides orphanages and a training centre in conjunction with the Ethiopian Orthodox Church. Our work in Somalia is suspended until the situation becomes more stable.

Monday in Holy Week—Cyprus and the Gulf, John E. Brown, Bishop. THANK GOD for many signs of spiritual growth in this ecumenical diocese; for the new ministry in the Yemen; and for the witness of many Christians of different traditions in isolated places in Arabia, and in the churches of Cyprus. PRAY for members of synod as they, with their church councils, consider the future structure and direction of the diocese.

Tuesday in Holy Week—Egypt, G.A. Malek, Bishop.

Wednesday in Holy Week—Iran, Iraj Mottahedeh, Bishop.

Maundy Thursday—Jerusalem, Archbishop Samir Kafity, Bishop.

Good Friday—PRAY for Christian-Jewish relations.

Holy Saturday—PRAY for the newly baptized and confirmed.

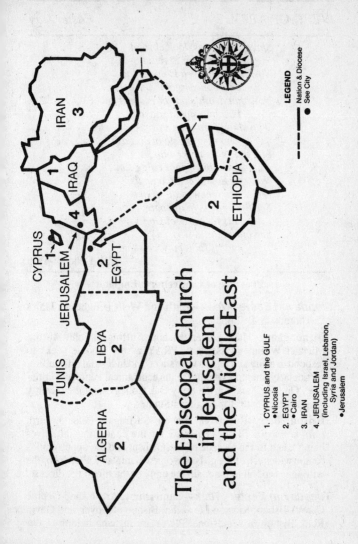

The Episcopal Church in Jerusalem and the Middle East

LEGEND

— Nation & Diocese
● See City
-·- Nation & Diocese

1. CYPRUS and the GULF
   ● Nicosia
2. EGYPT
   ● Cairo
3. IRAN
4. JERUSALEM
   (including Israel, Lebanon,
   Syria and Jordan)
   ● Jerusalem

IRAN 3

IRAQ 1 4

CYPRUS 1

JERUSALEM

EGYPT 2

ETHIOPIA 2

LIBYA 2

TUNIS

ALGERIA 2

37

> *Spread the news, look abroad,*
> *he has risen to reign.*
> *Now at last heaven is opened to*
> *earth once again.*
> *Now that death's power is spent and*
> *is vanquished for aye.*
> *Who should fear any storm,*
> *who now cringe in dismay?*
> *Lift your eyes to the hills,*
> *greet the bright rising sun.*
> *Now our hearts and our souls*
> *are renewed all as one.*
> *See the tomb is found bare,*
> *this the work of God's hand.*
> *See our Jesus now risen,*
> *in this faith may we stand.*

—H.B. Dehqani-Tafti

Province of Canterbury, England

Monday in Easter Week—Bath and Wells (England), James L. Thompson, Bishop.

Birmingham, Mark Santer, Bishop; Suffragan, John Austin; Michael Whinney, Assistant. PRAY as the diocese seeks to respond to a city and region with social and industrial difficulties, particularly unemployment; for the ecumenical Pentecost initiative "On Fire;" and for the Selly Oak Colleges and the recently established Centre for Anglican Studies.

Bristol, Barry Rogerson, Bishop; Suffragan, Peter J. Firth (*Malmesbury*). GIVE THANKS for the continuing initiatives being taken in the Decade of Evangelism and the opportunities for the wider use of the gifts of women in ministry. PRAY for the willingness of all to maintain the unity of the life of the diocese.

Tuesday in Easter Week—Canterbury, Archbishop George Carey, Bishop; Richard Llewellin, Bishop of Dover, and Gavin Reid, Bishop of Maidstone. PRAY for all who belong to our parish congregations, that each may discover his or her own ministry and calling; and for effective lay education and training.

Chelmsford, John Waine, Bishop; Area Bishops Michael Vickers (*Colchester*), Roger Sainsbury (*Barking*), Laurie Green (*Bradwell*). PRAY for the Diocesan Conferences for Clergy and Laity; for guidance in deploying ministerial resources across the diocese; and for relationships with people of other faiths.

Wednesday in Easter Week—**Chichester,** Eric Kemp, Bishop; Area Bishops John Hind (*Horsham*) and Ian Cunday (*Lewes*). PRAY for the work of the church in our rural parishes and for a better use of resources, that these small and often isolated communities may be revitalised and challenged by the gospel message; and for the continued unity of the church in this diocese. GIVE THANKS for Bishop Eric's 20 years of episcopal ministry among the people of East and West Sussex.

Coventry, Simon Barrington-Ward, Bishop; Suffragan, Clive Handford (*Warwick*). PRAY for the work of the Diocesan Spirituality Group and the Spirituality Adviser; for growth in relationship between urban and rural parishes; for new developments in lay training and in the summer school of clergy and laity; for the ministry of healing and for the growth of faith sharing; and for work in urban poverty and in tackling rural issues.

Derby, Peter S. Dawes, Bishop; Suffragan, Henry Richmond (*Repton*). GIVE THANKS for the faithful witness of clergy and people and for the expected ministry of women priests. PRAY for those who have doubts about this step and for a new ecumenical initiative.

Thursday in Easter Week—**Ely,** Stephen Sykes, Bishop, with Suffragan; W. Gordon Roe *(Huntingdon)*; and Assistant Bishop Michael Fisher, ssf. PRAY that the diocese may rise to the challenge of sustaining and encouraging its many small parishes in rural areas, and that there be a growth in lay participation in teams of ministry.

Gibraltar in the Diocese of Europe, Bishop to be chosen; Edward Holland, Suffragan, and Ambrose Weekes, Edmund Capper, Daniel de Pina Cabral, and Eric Devenport, Auxiliaries. PRAY for our new Diocesan Bishop as he takes up his responsibilities; and for new work in our diocese, especially in the cities of Eastern Europe and in relation to the European institutions.

Exeter, Hewlett Thompson, Bishop: Suffragans Peter Coleman (*Crediton*) and Richard Hawkins (*Plymouth*). PRAY for the clergy in this first year of our Ministry Review and Development scheme; and for laity's witness at their places of work and secular contact.

Friday in Easter Week—**Gloucester,** Bishop to be appointed; Jeremy Walsh, Suffragan. PRAY for new initiatives in ministry—for the Local Ministry Scheme; for women hoping to be ordained priest this year; and for those in non-stipendiary ministry. GIVE THANKS for an increasing response among young people to the claims of the gospel.

Guildford, Michael Adie, Bishop; Suffragan, David Wilcox (*Dorking*). PRAY for our ministry to London commuters; for deeper understanding and closer work with Christians of other traditions; for a richer spirituality in our congregations; and for clearer and more incisive witness and service to those in our localities.

Westminster Abbey, London; St. George's Chapel, Windsor. PRAY for their Deans, Michael Mayne and Patrick Mitchell, and for the Abbey's and Chapel's witness to millions of visitors from around the world; and for ministries through special services and events held in conjunction with interest groups and organisations.

Saturday in Easter Week—**Hereford,** John Oliver, Bishop; Bishop of Ludlow to be appointed. GIVE THANKS for the 1200th anniversary of the patron saint of Hereford Cathedral, St. Ethelbert; and for the response to our consultation on Patterns of Ministry and Pastoral Implications. PRAY for the ministry of the Bishop of Ludlow and for the work of Agricultural Chaplaincy pioneered in this diocese.

Leicester, Thomas F. Butler, Bishop.

The Church of England

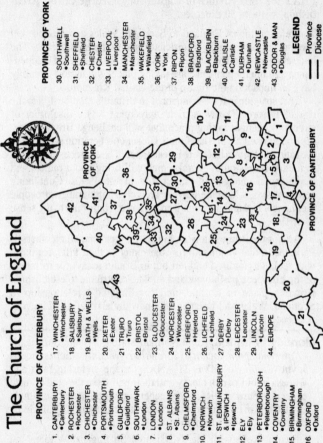

PROVINCE OF CANTERBURY

1. CANTERBURY
   • Canterbury
2. ROCHESTER
   • Rochester
3. CHICHESTER
   • Chichester
4. PORTSMOUTH
   • Portsmouth
5. GUILDFORD
   • Guildford
6. SOUTHWARK
   • London
7. LONDON
   • London
8. ST. ALBANS
   • St Albans
9. CHELMSFORD
   • Chelmsford
10. NORWICH
    • Norwich
11. ST. EDMUNDSBURY
    & IPSWICH
    • Ipswich
12. ELY
    • Ely
13. PETERBOROUGH
    • Peterborough
14. COVENTRY
    • Coventry
15. BIRMINGHAM
    • Birmingham
16. OXFORD
    • Oxford
17. WINCHESTER
    • Winchester
18. SALISBURY
    • Salisbury
19. BATH & WELLS
    • Wells
20. EXETER
    • Exeter
21. TRURO
    • Truro
22. BRISTOL
    • Bristol
23. GLOUCESTER
    • Gloucester
24. WORCESTER
    • Worcester
25. HEREFORD
    • Hereford
26. LICHFIELD
    • Lichfield
27. DERBY
    • Derby
28. LEICESTER
    • Leicester
29. LINCOLN
    • Lincoln
44. EUROPE

PROVINCE OF YORK

30. SOUTHWELL
    • Southwell
31. SHEFFIELD
    • Sheffield
32. CHESTER
    • Chester
33. LIVERPOOL
    • Liverpool
34. MANCHESTER
    • Manchester
35. WAKEFIELD
    • Wakefield
36. YORK
    • York
37. RIPON
    • Ripon
38. BRADFORD
    • Bradford
39. BLACKBURN
    • Blackburn
40. CARLISLE
    • Carlisle
41. DURHAM
    • Durham
42. NEWCASTLE
    • Newcastle
43. SODOR & MAN
    • Douglas

LEGEND

— Province
— Diocese
• See City

PRAY for the Province of Canterbury, George Carey, Archbishop, with its 30 dioceses.

The relationship of England to Scotland, Wales and Ireland will become an increasingly significant issue in the next decade. The huge changes throughout Europe, where new struggles of independence and interdependence are taking place, will almost certainly have an impact on the future of the United Kingdom.

That struggle is further mirrored in Britain's relationship to the rest of Europe. The Maastricht agreement was a disclosure of structural changes taking place that will challenge Britain's perception of itself as an island state. Closer co-operation is crucial to the future of Britain but there is resistance. The churches are caught in a deep recessionary spiral which will bring about radical and fundamental changes in church life in the 1990s. Continuing controversies, which are leaving an increasing number of people feeling isolated and marginalised, will also contribute to the sense of crisis.

PRAY for the Prime Minister, his government and all members of Parliament, that vision and foresight may be their gifts; for those who feel marginalised and left out in Britain today; for members of the European parliament and all who contribute to establishing Britain's place in Europe; and for England's relationship to Scotland, Wales and Ireland, for a new understanding of interdependence.

Monday: Lichfield, Keith Norman Sutton, Bishop; Suffragans (*Wolverhampton-vacant*), (*Shrewsbury-vacant*), Michael Scott-Joynt (*Stafford*). GIVE THANKS for the enduring faith and witness of our parish clergy and their people in the cold climate of secular Europe. PRAY for deeper commitment to the example of St. Chad in making new disciples in partnership with all God's people in the West Midlands.

Lincoln, Robert M. Hardy, Bishop; Suffragans, William Ind (*Grantham*) and David Tustin (*Grimsby*); and Assistant Bishops Gerald Colin, Dick Darby and Richard Cutts. PRAY for a deeper commitment to Christian stewardship and for pastoral re-organization in the diocese.

London, David Hope, Bishop; Area Bishops Brian Masters (*Edmonton*), John Hughes (*Kensington*), Richard Chartres (*Stepney*), and Graham Dow (*Willesden*); Suffragan John Klyberg (*Fulham*); and Assistant Bishops Maurice Wood and Michael Marshall. PRAY for the life and work of the parishes throughout the diocese; for the life of the church schools and all who teach in them. GIVE THANKS for the signs of new life and all who will be confirmed this year.

Tuesday: Norwich, Peter Nott, Bishop; Suffragans David Bentley (*Lynn*) and Hugo de Waal (*Thetford*). PRAY for openness to radical changes in patterns of ministry.

Oxford, Richard D. Harries, Bishop.

Peterborough, William John Westwood, Bishop; Suffragan, Paul Barber (*Brixworth*). PRAY for blessing on our Council for Evangelism; on initiatives in lay training; on our link with the Diocese of Down and Dromore; and, above all else, for a growth in the practice of Christian stewardship.

Wednesday: Portsmouth, Timothy Bavin, Bishop. GIVE THANKS for the ministry of women in the diocese. PRAY for laity as well as clergy as they come to terms with and work out the implications of the Church of England's decision to ordain women to the priesthood.

Rochester (England), Michael Turnbull, Bishop. PRAY for the newly appointed Suffragan Bishop of Tonbridge; for continued support for, and the use of, the Bishop's Mission Fund; and for deepening links with the Diocese of Harare.

Saint Albans, John B. Taylor, Bishop; Suffragans, (*Bedford—vacant*), Robin Smith (*Hertford*). PRAY for our two diocesan missionaries in their task of training in evangelism and inducting parish missions; and for new patterns of ministerial and theological education which are emerging.

Thursday: St. Edmundsbury and Ipswich, John Dennis, Bishop; Suffragan for *Dunwich,* Jonathan Bailey. PRAY for the diocesan needs of ministry, not least through the growth of the local non-stipendiary ministry.

Salisbury, Diocesan Bishop to be chosen; Area Bishops, John Kirkham (*Sherborne*) and Peter Vaughan (*Ramsbury*); Honorary Bishop, John Cavell. GIVE THANKS for deepening faith, and openness to new patterns of lay and ordained ministry. PRAY for the new Diocesan Bishop.

Friday: **Southwark,** Roy Williamson, Bishop; Area Bishops Wilfred Wood (*Croydon*), Martin Wharton (*Kingston*) and Peter Hall (*Woolwich*). PRAY for the new bishop of Kingston.

Truro (England), Michael Thomas Ball, Bishop.

Saturday: **Winchester (England),** Colin C.W. James, Bishop; Suffragans Michael Manktelow *(Basingstoke)* and John F. Perry *(Southampton)*; Assistant Bishops Leslie Lloyd-Rees and H.B. Dehqani-Tafti. PRAY for the development of collaborative ministries, the renewal of personal witness, and a growth in sacrificial giving.

Worcester (England), Philip H.E. Goodrich, Bishop; Suffragan (*Dudley—vacant*). PRAY that there may be a committed core of people in the diocese with vision and concern to reach out to people beyond the church. PRAY for the coherence of the church in the diocese.

Show me, O Lord, your mercy, and delight my heart with it. Let me find you whom I so longingly seek. See, here is the man whom the robbers seized, mishandled, and left half dead on the road to Jericho. O kind-hearted Samaritan, come to my aid! I am the sheep who wandered into the wilderness—seek after me, and bring me home again to your fold. Do with me what you will, that I may stay by you all the days of my life, and praise you with all those who are with you in heaven for all eternity.

(St. Jerome)

PRAY for the Anglican Church of the Southern Cone (Iglesia Anglicana del Cono Sur de las Americas), Colin F. Bazley, Presiding Bishop, with its six dioceses; and for the Church of the Province of Melanesia, Amos S. Waiaru, Archbishop, with its six dioceses.

There are 27,000 members in the Anglican Church of the Southern Cone, in the dioceses of Argentina, Chile, Bolivia, Peru, Paraguay and Uruguay, covering 2,440,000 square miles. Approximately 80 million people live in the area, 76 percent of whom claim allegiance to the Roman Catholic Church. Founded in 1983, the Province is served by 150 clergy in 265 churches. There has been an extensive medical, educational, agricultural and social outreach in rural and urban areas.

Anglicanism grew from the influx of British immigrants who came to South America during the 19th century and continued with missionary activities among indigenous peoples, pioneered by Captain Allen Gardiner. In later years churches have been planted in the major cities. The South American Missionary Society continues this work today.

There are 250 Anglican clergy in 100 parish districts serving the 120,000 Anglicans living in the 16,700 square miles covering the Province of Melanesia, which extends over the Solomon Islands, Vanuatu, and New Caledonia. Over 50 percent of the population are Christians. The Anglican presence in Melanesia dates from 1849 when Bishop George Selwyn of New Zealand toured the islands and brought back some young Melanesians to his school in Auckland. John Patteson became the first Bishop in 1861 and was martyred ten years later. The first station was on Norfold Island, but permanent stations were founded in the 1880s. The Melanesian Brotherhood, a religious order, was founded in 1925. The Province became autonomous in 1975. The Provincial Offices are in the Solomon Islands and the church is served by the Church of Melanesia Newsletter and the Bishop Patteson Theological Centre.

GIVE THANKS for the work of the Melanesia Board of Mission and the sending of missionaries to Fiji, Papua New Guinea, Australia and England. PRAY for the ministry to youth.

LEGEND

—— Diocese
- - - Nation
● See City

Igreja Episcopal do Brasil

7. CENTRAL
   ● Rio de Janeiro
8. NORTHERN
   ● Recife
9. SOUTHERN
   ● Porto Alegre
10. SOUTH CENTRAL
    ● Sao Paulo
11. SOUTHWESTERN
    ● Santa Maria
12. BRASILIA
    ● Brasilia
13. PELOTAS
    ● Pelotas

Falkland Islands
(See of Canterbury)

Iglesia Anglicana del Cono Sur de America

1. ARGENTINA
   ● Buenos Aires
2. CHILE
   ● Santiago
3. NORTHERN ARGENTINA
   ● Salta
4. PARAGUAY
   ● Asuncion
5. PERU with BOLIVA
   ● Lima
6. URUGUAY
   ● Montevideo

Monday: Argentina (Province of the Southern Cone), David Leake, Bishop.

Chile, Presiding Bishop Colin F. Bazley, Bishop; Ian Morrison, Assistant. PRAY for perseverence in the task of evangelism and church planting, especially in cities of the North; for discipleship-training that puts everyone to work and to pray; for future episcopal ministry; for progress in inter-church relationships; and for the President who took office in March.

Tuesday: Northern Argentina, Maurice Sinclair, Bishop; Mario Marino, Assistant. PRAY for the extension of Anglican witness into Jujuy and Tucuman; for ministry among young people, especially in the Amer-Indian communities; for the granting of land rights; and in everything openness to the Holy Spirit.

Paraguay, John Ellison, Bishop.

Wednesday: Peru with Bolivia, Alan Winstanley, Bishop. PRAY for sustained growth, both spiritual and numerical, and increasing maturity among clergy and leaders.

Uruguay, William Godfrey, Bishop. GIVE THANKS to God for five years as a diocese; for ministry amongst the very poor; for our social outreach programmes; for the strengthening of congregational life; for the Christian education work; for the seminary as it seeks to develop local Uruguayan ministry; and for the Bishop, that he may be led by God as the diocese seeks to discern His will.

Thursday: Central Melanesia (Province of Melanesia), Archbishop Amos S. Waiaru, Bishop. GIVE THANKS for the launching of the Decade of Evangelism and renewal in the diocese and for commitment of time, effort, and life to Jesus Christ. PRAY for the Diocesan Office for Evangelism and Renewal for the work of the Coordinator in the diocese; and for plans for the establishment of a Training Centre for the diocese at Longgu District.

Hanuato'o, James Philip Mason, Bishop. GIVE THANKS for the blessing God has poured on this diocese. PRAY for St. Stephen's High School, Pamua; for the Melanesian Brothers Section Household at Fox Household and the work of their companions; for the Mothers' Union and their ministry, especially St. George Kindergarten; for development projects; and for the Rev. Richard Teona, co-ordinator for evangelism, renewal and youth ministry.

Friday: Malaita, R. Aumae, Bishop.

Temotu, Lazarus S. Munamua, Bishop. THANK GOD for the ministry of four religious communities in the Province. PRAY for a greater involvement and participation of the laity in evangelism and renewal ministries in the villages.

Saturday: Vanuatu, H. Tavoa, Bishop.

Ysabel, E. Pogo, Bishop.

Province of Melanesia

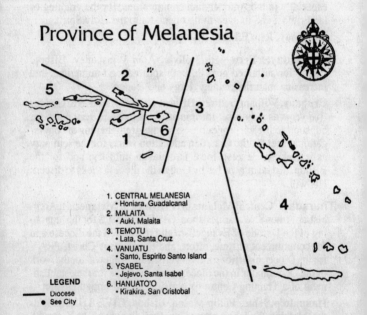

1. CENTRAL MELANESIA
   • Honiara, Guadalcanal
2. MALAITA
   • Auki, Malaita
3. TEMOTU
   • Lata, Santa Cruz
4. VANUATU
   • Santo, Espirito Santo Island
5. YSABEL
   • Jejevo, Santa Isabel
6. HANUATO'O
   • Kirakira, San Cristobal

LEGEND
— Diocese
• See City

PRAY for the province of Dublin, Donald Caird, Archbishop, with its five dioceses.

In a population of 4,925,000, over 4,000,800 call themselves Christians with 70 percent being Roman Catholic and 20 percent Protestant. The geographical area covers 32,597 square miles. The Republic of Ireland and Northern Ireland have 12 dioceses grouped in the Provinces of Armagh and Dublin. Approximately 1,200 parishes and over 650 clergy minister to the needs of the faithful. The Church of Ireland Theological College is located in Dublin.

Tracing its origins to St. Patrick and his companions in the fifth century, the Irish Church has been marked by strong missionary efforts. In 1537 the English king was declared head of the Church of Ireland and allegiance to Rome was forbidden. Although Anglicanism received state support most Irish Christians maintained loyalty to Rome. In 1870 the church was dis-established and continued as an independent Province. It is governed by a General Synod with a House of Bishops and a House of Representatives, the Archbishop of Armagh being elected by the House of Bishops from their own number.

Monday *(St. Mark)*—**Cashel and Ossory,** Noel Willoughby, Bishop. PRAY for the deepening of spiritual life and for the pursuit of true priorities.

Tuesday: Cork, Cloyne and Ross, Robert Warke, Bishop. In a predominantly Roman Catholic area PRAY for inter-church relations both at parochial and diocesan levels, that vision and courage may be shown. GIVE THANKS for the supportive ministry of retired clergy.

Wednesday: Dublin and Glendalough, Archbishop Donald Caird, Bishop.

Thursday: Limerick and Killaloe, Edward Darling, Bishop. GIVE THANKS for ministry to tourists who visit our scenic diocese. PRAY that those isolated people in our remote rural areas may be encouraged and strengthened by the support of prayer from their fellow Anglicans throughout the world.

Friday: Meath and Kildare, Walton N.F. Empey, Bishop. PRAY for continued dialogue between political leaders in Northern Ireland and the Republic of Ireland so that peace may come to our land. GIVE THANKS for the fruitful link which we have with the Diocese of Bethlehem, Pennsylvania.

Saturday: PRAY for Anglican bishops, priests, and deacons throughout the world.

Church
of
Ireland

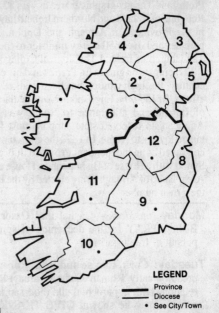

LEGEND

━━ Province
── Diocese
● See City/Town

PROVINCE OF ARMAGH

1. ARMAGH
   ● Armagh
2. CLOGHER
   ● Fivemiletown
3. CONNOR
   ● Belfast
4. DERRY AND RAPHOE
   ● Londonderry
5. DOWN AND DROMORE
   ● South Belfast
6. KILMORE, ELPHIN AND ARDAGH
   ● Cavan
7. TUAM KILLALA AND ACHONRY
   ● Crossmolina

PROVINCE OF DUBLIN

8. DUBLIN AND GLENDALOUGH
   ● Dublin
9. CASHEL AND OSSORY
   ● Kilkenny
10. CORK CLOYNE AND ROSS
    ● Cork
11. LIMERICK AND KILLALOE
    ● Limerick
12. MEATH AND KILDARE
    ● Maynooth

50

PRAY for Igreja Episcopal Anglicana do Brasil, Claudio V. S. Gastal, Primate, with its seven dioceses.

The Episcopal Anglican Church of Brazil doesn't want to be just another church amidst 150 million Brazilians. She is attempting to find her place in this country, almost half the area of Latin America, where Portuguese is spoken. She wants to be faithful to the Anglican ethos and knows that her singular contribution will be to find expression for this ethos in the daily life of the church, in Brazilian context.

At the same time she also knows that her participation in the *Missio Dei* requires a global view, where everything connects. To proclaim the Good News, to feed the faithful people, to serve the poor, to change the unjust social structures and to fight for the life and integrity of the creation is that holistic task. *How to you do it? How to be obedient to the Lord?*

The external debt, the multitude of poor and those oppressed by a system which benefits only 10 percent of the population, the precariousness of survival of millions of Brazilians (even within our own church), the multitude of children on the streets, of workers without land ... are challenges which shake the church into facing the responsibility of being more than a sign of the presence of God among men and women.

PRAY for the Episcopal Anglican Church of Brazil and its new Primate, spiritual and pastoral leader of the seven dioceses. GIVE THANKS to God for the ministry and life of the late Archbishop Olavo Luiz, who led the church for the last seven years.

Map, p. 46.

Monday *(St. Philip and St. James)*—**Brasilia,** Almir dos Santos, Bishop.

Central Brazil, Sydney A. Rùiz, Bishop. PRAY for more vocations; for spiritual growth, evangelistic outreach and church planting; for witness and service through our pastoral and educational programmes; and for a deeper commitment in the bond of Christian unity, faith and love.

Tuesday: **Northern Brazil,** Clovis E. Rodrigues, Bishop. PRAY for new frontiers; for theological education; and for new commitment to the popular struggle for justice.

Wednesday: **Pelotas,** Luiz Prado, Bishop. PRAY for our calling and discipleship; for commitment to very deprived people: landless groups, street-children, urban poor in the slums, fishermen and small farmers; for the challenge of political transformation; and for young people and our environment, mainly Taim, our local ecological reserve.

Thursday: Sao Paulo, (formerly South Central Brazil), Glauco Soares de Lima, Bishop. Our new name is the name of our see city, a megalopolis, an urban area of 15 million people, a microcosm of all the world's problems. PRAY for this city; for our ten candidates for ordained ministry; and that we attain our outreach goals—help to street children, AIDS victims and the elderly.

Friday: **Southern Brazil,** Archbishop Claudio V.S. Gastal, Bishop.

Saturday: **Southwestern Brazil,** Jubal Neves, Bishop-elect. PRAY for the new bishop and for the solidarity of the diocesan people with all those who are suffering and are in necessity; and for evangelisation as a concrete signal of Christ's presence among our people.

> *From needing danger, to be good,*
> *From owing you yesterday's tears today,*
> *From trusting so much in your blood,*
> *That in that hope, we wound our soul away,*
> *From bribing you with alms, to excuse*
> *Some sin more burdenous,*
> *From light affecting, in religion, news,*
> *From thinking us all soul, neglecting thus*
> *Our mutual duties, Lord deliver us.*

(John Donne)

PRAY for the (Anglican) Council of Churches of East Asia, Moses Tay, President, with its six dioceses.

Pending the establishment of new Provinces in the area, the Council of Churches of East Asia serves as a link among the dioceses of Hong Kong and Macao, Kuching (Borneo), Sabah, Singapore, Taiwan and West Malaysia. Discussions continue toward autonomy in Hong Kong and Macao. There are a number of dioceses which come under the metropolitical authority of the Archbishop of Canterbury and are united in the Council.

Although autonomous, the Philippine Episcopal Church, the Philippine Independent Church, the Church in Myanmar and the Church in Australia are members of the Council.

Map not available.

Monday: **Hong Kong and Macao,** Peter Kong-kit Kwong, Bishop. PRAY that the church may continue to be a faithful witness to the gospel in a time of transition, that we may bring hope, encouragement and comfort to the people here. PRAY for the guidance of the Holy Spirit as we undertake the transition of the diocese into a Province.

Tuesday: **Kuching, Sarawak (Malaysia)** John Leong Chee Yun, Bishop; Made Katib, Assistant. THANK GOD for the continual church population growth of 5,000 per annum; for His grace and blessing on our work to spread the good news to all people in Sarawak and Brunei Darussalam; and for His guidance and enhancement to our Theological College, the House of the Epiphany, in the training of more priests for the Divine Ministry. PRAY for our laity, which plays an extremely important role in evangelism and outreach to those who clamour to come into contact with our Lord Jesus Christ.

Wednesday: **Sabah (Malaysia),** Yong Ping Chung, Bishop. GIVE THANKS for the HARVEST toward 2000 programme in 1993 in our diocese. PRAY for doubling and redoubling of the number of Anglicans, clergy, parish workers, evangelists and youth evangelists in the diocese to the year 2000; and for every Anglican to have the joy of leading a person to Christ in 1994.

Thursday *(The Ascension)*—**Singapore**, Moses Tay, Bishop. PRAY for speedy evangelization of the 300 million people in the six countries of the diocese; for the Dean of Thailand and Laos, the Rev. Dr. Monty Morris; the Dean of Cambodia, the Rev. Dr. John Benson; the Dean of Vietnam, the Ven. John Tan; and the Dean of Indonesia, Canon James Wong. PRAY for our zeal and faithfulness in personal witness and evangelism; for social concern and justice, and the clear identity of this nation in the world community.

Friday: **PRAY for victims of HIV/AIDS and those who minister to them.**

Saturday: **West Malaysia,** John G. Savarimuthu, Bishop.

Province of the Indian Ocean

LEGEND
— Diocese
● See City

1. ANTANANARIVO
   ● Antananarivo
2. ANTSIRANANA
   ● Antsiranana
3. MAURITIUS
   ● Port Louis
4. SEYCHELLES
   ● Victoria
5. TOAMASINA
   ● Toamasina

PRAY for the Province of the Indian Ocean, French Chang-Him, Archbishop, with its five dioceses.

The countries of Madagasgar, Mauritius, and Seychelles comprise the 230,223 square miles of this Province, founded in 1973. Of the total populationof 9,767,000, 5,082,000 are Christians, 83,000 Anglicans.

GIVE THANKS for blessings during the past 21 years. PRAY that the Province's future will continue to be guided.

Monday: Antananarivo (Madagasgar), Remi J. Rabenirina, Bishop. THANK GOD for the 10 new churches and three other new congregations, first visible results of the Decade of Evangelism. PRAY for sufficient and adequate equipment and means of transport for all clergy; and for the growth of the new Anglican Community at Morondava.

Tuesday: Antsiranana, Keith J. Benzies, Bishop. GIVE THANKS for the publication of the Diocesan Hymnal and the great increase in literacy; PRAY for the Diocesan Farm Project, developing young people's skills in modern humane farming methods.

Wednesday: Mauritius, Rex Donat, Bishop. PRAY for guidance of the Holy Spirit as the diocese elaborates a project of training for laity and eventual ordinands.

Thursday: Seychelles, Archbishop French Chang-Him, Bishop. GIVE THANKS for the witness and ministry of children, youth and women in this diocese. PRAY that the majority of men in the church and in society may rediscover their calling and mission and renew their commitment.

Friday: Toamasina, D. W. Smith, Bishop.

Saturday: PRAY for religious orders.

PRAY for the province of the Pacific, Episcopal Church USA, Mrs. Marion Cedarblade, President, with its 18 dioceses.

Map, pp. 22-23.

Monday: Alaska, Steven Charleston, Bishop. PRAY that the light of our witness to Christ Jesus may continue to shine brightly in our diocese. GIVE THANKS for the powerful presence of the Holy Spirit raising up the church in Alaska.

Arizona, Robert R. Shahan, Bishop. GIVE THANKS for our new diocesan and his leadership as we develop a new vision for Arizona. PRAY for the decentralization that is in progress; for our willingness to accept change as we work toward a greater sense of "openness" in this vast and diverse diocese; and for the ministry of the laity and clergy.

California, William E. Swing, Bishop. PRAY for the African-American Economic Development Task Force, for the Vision 2000 Commission; for construction of housing units for Hispanic immigrants, of Grace Cathedral's Chapter House, of a Seafarers Chapel, of a Life-Case facility, and of El Rancho del Obispo lodges. PRAY for help in the AIDS epidemic.

Eastern Oregon, Rustin R. Kimsey, Bishop. GIVE THANKS for fragile gifts of persons, forests, mountains, rivers and desert. PRAY for vision to see the face of Jesus in the whole creation; for the will to honor and support each other in our baptismal ministries; for the courage to structure our common life simply and faithfully; and for the trust that all will be well.

Tuesday: El Camino Real, Richard L. Shimpfky, Bishop.

Hawaii, Donald Hart, Bishop. PRAY for people to give leadership through reconciliation, peacemaking, and servanthood; for vocations among our ethnic groups; and for witness to our oneness in Christ while respecting racial diversity. GIVE THANKS for a calling to share the gospel; and for the Diocesan Institute training program.

Idaho, John S. Thornton, Bishop. PRAY that we will grow more and more into the likeness of Christ and that we will incarnate his love among all the people with whom we live, especially children and youth and the poor and homeless.

Los Angeles, Frederick H. Borsch, Bishop; Chester L. Talton, Suffragan. PRAY for healing and reconciliation; for our invitation to peoples of many backgrounds to join in our communities of faith; for our youth ministries; and for the building and mission of our new Cathedral Center.

Wednesday: Navajoland, Steven T. Plummer, Bishop. PRAY for our Bishop; for ministry to our youth; for guidance of the Holy Spirit to continue evangelism and growth; and for leadership and the calling process for our people in the ordained ministry. GIVE THANKS for help in stewardship and for the work of the church in this area mission.

Nevada, Steward C. Zabriskie, Bishop. PRAY for the ministry of the Paiute Indians on the Pyramid Lake Reservation; for the renewal of Galilee Camp and Conference Center; for our ministries to the poor and homeless; and for our continued growth in understanding and doing the ministry of all the baptized.

Northern California, Jerry A. Lamb, Bishop. PRAY for the establishment of new congregations; for the development of significant cross-cultural ministry during the Decade of Evangelism; and for the financial and personnel resources to carry out these ministries.

Olympia, Vincent W. Warner, Bishop. PRAY for the Diocese of Olympia as we, with the larger church throughout the world, seek to become one people of God who proclaim boldly by word and action the reconciling Gospel of Jesus Christ.

Thursday *(St. Augustine of Canterbury)*—**PRAY for George Carey, Archbishop of Canterbury.**

Friday: Oregon, Robert L. Ladehoff, Bishop. GIVE THANKS for our growing outreach ministries. PRAY for our camp and conference programs; for our programs of evangelism and stewardship; and for an increase in lay vocations.

San Diego, Gethin B. Hughes, Bishop. PRAY for missionary expansion of the diocese, which covers part of the nation's fastest growing area; and for the expansion of ethnic ministries in this cross-cultural diocese.

San Joaquin, John-David M. Schofield, Bishop. GIVE THANKS for the work among youth in the Diocese and an increase of young people who will commit their lives to Jesus Christ. PRAY for an increased number of clergy and lay leaders among Hispanics, Filipinos, and Southeast Asians.

Saturday: Spokane, Frank Jeffrey Terry, Bishop. PRAY for our newly emerging regional ministries and a new sense of mission as our diocese begins its second 100 years.

Taiwan, John Chieh-Tsung Chien, Bishop.

Utah, George E. Bates, Bishop. PRAY for commitment to witness boldly in our communities to the power and mercy of God in Christ; and to exercise the gifts we have been given for ministry. GIVE THANKS for the many gifts bestowed upon this diocese.

Guam and Micronesia, under the jurisdiction of the American Presiding Bishop and his designate, the Rt. Rev. Donald Hart, Hawaii. PRAY for unity and vision for the work of Christ. GIVE THANKS for the love, respect, and hospitality of the peoples on these islands.

> *O God, who has bound us together in this bundle of life, give us grace to understand how our lives depend upon the courage, the industry, the honesty and the integrity of our fellow men, that we may be mindful of their needs, grateful for their faithfulness, and faithful in our responsibilities to them; through Jesus Christ our Lord.*

PRAY for the Church of South India, Vasant P. Dandin, Moderator, with its 21 dioceses.

The Church of South India is the oldest United Church and the first to bring together Christians from Episcopal and non-Episcopal traditions. After 20 years of negotiation the Church of South India was inaugurated in 1947, bringing together Christians from the Anglican, Methodist, Presbyterian, Congregationalist and Reformed traditions.

Monday: Coimbatore, William Moses, Bishop.

Dornakal, D. Noah Samuel, Bishop.

East Kerala, K.J. Samuel, Bishop.

Jaffna, David Jeyaratnam Ambalavanar, Bishop.

Tuesday *(The Visitation)*—**Kanyakumari,** G. Christdhas, Bishop.

Karimnagar, K.E. Swamidas, Bishop.

Karnataka Central, C.D. Jathanna, Bishop.

Karnataka North, Moderator V.P. Dandin, Bishop.

Wednesday: Karnataka South, Deva Prasad Shettian, Moderator's Commissary.

Krishna-Godavari, T.B.D. Prakasa Rao, Bishop.

Madhya Kerala, M.C. Mani, Bishop. PRAY for the Bishop and the continued commitment of clergy and laity, especially youth, to the mission of the church; for the Retreat Centre which is being built; and for the election of the new Diocesan Bishop.

Thursday: Madras, Mazilimani Azariah, Bishop.

Madurai-Ramnad, D.Pothirajulu, Bishop.

Medak, Victor Premasagar, Bishop.

Nandyal.

Friday: North Kerala, Dr. P.G. Kruvilla, Bishop.

Rayalseema, L.V. Azariah, Bishop.

South Kerala, Dr. Samuel Amirtham, Bishop.

Saturday: **Tiruchirapalli-Thanjavur,** R. Paulraj, Bishop.

Tirunelveli, Jason S. Dharmaraj, Bishop. PRAISE GOD for the social welfare and the flood relief programmes. PRAY for the lay training and counselling programmes; for the outreach ministry within the diocese and in the northern part of the country through the Indian Missionary Society.

Vellore, R. Trinity Bhaskeran, Bishop.

United Churches

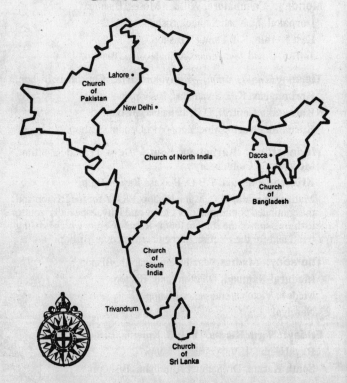

PRAY for the province of Western Australia, Peter F. Carnley, Archbishop, with its three dioceses.

Map, p. 28.

Monday: **Bunbury,** Hamish Jamieson, Bishop. THANK GOD for the "discipleship" way of training for ministry, both clergy and lay. PRAY that a real breakthrough will occur in recognising our need and dependence upon Jesus, not on our own resources, and that we would be led by the Holy Spirit, not our own imaginings.

Tuesday: **North West Australia,** Anthony Howard Nichols, Bishop.

Perth, Archbishop Peter F. Carnley, Bishop; Brian Kyme, David Murray and Brian Farran, Assistants. PRAY that we may be at the forefront in dealing with such issues as justice, sexuality and the breaking down of barriers; and for our Vision for the 90s, as we aim to open 40 new parishes within 10 years.

Province of York, England

Wednesday: **Blackburn (England),** Alan Chesters, Bishop; Suffragans, Jack Nicholls (*Lancaster*) and (*Burnley, vacant*). GIVE THANKS for the witness to the gospel of faithful lay people and clergy. PRAY FOR continuing unity within the diocese; for the new Bishop of Burnley; for the Mission Audit of the diocese; for the work of the church in deprived areas; for church schools as they seek the right way forward in the areas of financing and management; and for good relations with other faith communities.

Bradford (England), David J. Smith, Bishop. PRAY for our concern to reach out to the unchurched and to relate with those of other faiths in our city; and for 1994 as we celebrate seventy-five years as a diocese.

Thursday: Carlisle (England), Ian Harland, Bishop.

Chester (England), Michael Baughen, Bishop; Suffragans Michael Langrish (*Birkenhead*) and Frank Sargeant (*Stockport*). PRAY for the developing initiatives in youth work across the diocese.

Friday: Durham (England), David E. Jenkins, Bishop. PRAY that the clergy and people of the diocese will seek to pursue in partnership the initiatives and opportunities being presented to them.

Saturday *(St. Barnabas)*—**Liverpool (England),** David S. Sheppard, Bishop; Suffragan, Michael Henshall (*Warrington*); Graham Chadwick and Jim Roxburgh, Assistants. THANK GOD for the healing of old sectarian bitterness. PRAY for local churches who have entered into ecumenical covenants; and for witness to Christ's hope, especially where large-scale unemployment is two generations deep.

Blessed are all your saints, O God and King, who have traveled over the tempestuous sea of this life and have made the harbor of peace and felicity. Watch over us who are still on our dangerous voyage; and remember those who lie exposed to the rough storms of trouble and temptations. Frail is our vessel, and the ocean is wide; but as in our mercy you have set our course, so steer the vessel of our life towards the everlasting shore of peace, and bring us at length to the quiet haven of our heart's desire, where you, O God, are blessed and live and reign for ever

(St. Augustine of Hippo)

PRAY for the province of York, Church of England, John S. Habgood, Primate, with its 14 dioceses.

Like other parts of the Anglican Communion, England is suffering from the effects of the economic recession and the social and political strains these bring. It is also working through the issues arising from its membership of the European Community.

The Church of England is facing up to the challenge of being the national church in a pluralist, multi-faith, increasingly secular society. It is also seeking for ways to deal generously and sensitively with the consequences of its decision to ordain women to the priesthood.

Map, p. 41. Intercessions begin on p. 61.

Monday: Manchester, Christopher J. Mayfield, Bishop; Colin Scott and David Bonser, Suffragans. From Manchester's Vision Statement: "We seek to offer worship which honours God, uplifts worshippers, reflects the community, and attracts newcomers." PRAY that we may express God's love by challenging and helping to change unjust structures locally and worldwide.

Newcastle, Alec Graham, Bishop; Kenneth Gill, Assistant. PRAY for workers in inner-city parishes; for wisdom in promoting ecumenical cooperation; for adult education; and that congregations in the diocese be helped to turn outwards in mission and evangelism.

Tuesday: Ripon, David Young, Bishop; Suffragan, Malcolm Menin (*Knaresborough*). PRAY for the new Diocesan Missioner and the parishes responding to the challenge to be effective in evangelisation; and for the successful completion of the Bishop's Appeal.

Wednesday: Sheffield, David Ramsay Lunn, Bishop; Michael Gear, (*Doncaster*). PRAY that there may be sufficient generosity of spirit to preserve our unity as we move towards the ordination of women to the priesthood. Please continue to PRAY for the growing numbers who have no work.

Thursday: Sodor and Man, Noel Jones, Bishop. PRAY for closer ecumenical co-operation; for the development of lay leadership; and for smaller rural parishes finding difficulties in meeting financial challenges.

Southwell, Patrick Harris, Bishop; Alan Morgan, Suffragan. Throughout the diocese, deaneries have been planning their strategy for the future. GIVE THANKS for the unity of the diocese and PRAY that we may express this in practical collaboration and shared ministry.

Friday: Wakefield, Nigel McCulloch, Bishop; John Finney (*Pontefract*). PRAY for congregations to grow, the faith to be taught, giving to increase, and communities to be served in the name of the Lord.

Saturday: York, Archbishop John Habgood, Bishop; Suffragans, Donald Snelgrove (*Hull*), Gordon Bates (*Whitby*) and Humphrey Taylor (*Selby*). PRAY that the church may have the wisdom and courage to respond to the needs of a changing society, not least in relation to Europe; for our companion diocese of Mechelen in Brussels; and for developing relationships with the church in Poland.

O Jesus, my feet are dirty. Come even as a slave to me, pour water into your bowl, come and wash my feet. In asking such a thing I know I am overbold, but I dread what was threatened when you said to me, "If I do not wash your feet I have no fellowship with you." Wash my feet then, because I long for your companionship. And yet, what am I asking? It was well for Peter to ask you to wash his feet; for him that was all that was needed for him to be clean in every part. With me it is different; though you wash me now I shall still stand in need of that other washing, the cleansing you promised when you said, "there is a baptism I must needs be baptized with."

(Origen of Alexandria)

PRAY for the Province of Southern Africa, Desmond Tutu, Metropolitan, with its 22 dioceses.

The church in Southern Africa has always been involved in the struggle for liberation, taking our Lord's own example (Luke 4:17-21). The changing circumstances in South Africa have a chain effect on the rest of the subcontinent, since the neighbouring states of Lesotho, Swaziland, Namibia and Mozambique have all been victims of the policy of destabilization. The role of the church has to undergo change as we grapple with new forms of ministry in these changing circumstances. True democracy demands constant vigilance and the church cannot align itself with any political movement.

> *Praise be to you Lord God*
> *for you make all things new*
> *in Jesus Christ;*
> *By the power of your Spirit*
> *renew our humanity,*
> *heal our brokenness*
> *and set your Church free*
> *truly to live and love in Jesus.*

Monday: **Bloemfontein (South Africa),** Thomas S. Stanage, Bishop. PRAY for those training for ministry at theological college and the University of the Orange Free State; for a continuing focus on evangelism and formation in the Decade of Evangelism; and for ministry in a situation of economic hardship and political change.

Cape Town (South Africa), Archbishop Desmond Tutu, Bishop; Edward MacKenzie and Geoff Quinlan, Bishops-Suffragan. GIVE THANKS for the ministry of Bishop Charles Albertyn (retired). PRAY that the division of the diocese may lead to renewed ministry of the whole people of God, especially through the RENEW programme; and that the young people may be empowered to be effective in bringing about reconciliation and building basic Christian Communities.

Christ the King (South Africa), Peter John Lee, Bishop. GIVE

THANKS for signs of stabilisation in South African society. PRAY for the process of reconstruction and for the church's role in caring, preaching the gospel and peacemaking within that process.

Tuesday: George (South Africa), D. C. Damant, Bishop. PRAY for the guidance of the Holy Spirit in all our planning for evangelism and development, and in community relations, as we look forward to playing our full role in a more just and democratic society.

Grahamstown (South Africa), David P.H. Russell, Bishop. GIVE THANKS for the election of a Suffragan Bishop in succession to Eric Pike, translated to Port Elizabeth as Diocesan Bishop in June 1993; and for South Africa's progress towards a non-racial democracy. PRAY for the ministry of peace-making and witness for justice in a period of transition and political change; for the strengthening of ministries to the victims of economic injustice where black unemployment is as high as 80 percent in many areas; for the reconstruction of the Rural Development Programme; for pioneering a new model for theological education by the Rector, staff and students of the College of the Transfiguration.

Johannesburg (South Africa), Duncan Buchanan, Bishop. GIVE THANKS for continued growth in commitment and ministry. PRAY for the church's role as peacemaker in the midst of violence and political transition; and for the diocesan commitment to being a more caring community.

Wednesday: Kimberly and Kuruman (South Africa), Niongokulu Winston Ndungane, Bishop. THANK GOD for faithful clergy and people. PRAY for guidance of the Holy Spirit in our five-year development programme; and for the availability of resources financial and human for effective ministry in the diocese.

Klerksdorp (South Africa), David C.T. Nkwe, Bishop. PRAY for more vocations to the ordained ministry; for acceptance of the Renew Program; for relief from the drought; and for employment opportunities for all the unemployed.

Lebombo (Mozambique), Dinis S. Sengulane, Bishop. THANK GOD for the restoration of peace in the country; for the vision which characterised the celebration of the centenary of the diocese; and for the congregations founded in the context of the centenary. PRAY for the work of rebuilding Maciene Centre; and for those who were ordained in the centenary year.

Thursday: Lesotho, Philip S. Mokuku, Bishop.

Namibia, James H. Kauluma, Bishop.

Natal (South Africa), Michael Nuttall, Bishop; Matthew Makhaye and Ross Cuthbertson, Suffragans. PRAY for an end to political violence in our society; and for the church's ministry in expanding informal settlements, especially around Durban, which is one of the fastest growing cities in the world.

Niassa (Mozambique), Paulino T. Manhique, Bishop.

Port Elizabeth (South Africa), Eric Pike, Bishop. GIVE THANKS for the eighteen-year episcopate of former Bishop Bruce Read Evans, retired with motor neurone disease. PRAY for Bishop Evans and his family; and for the new Bishop and his leadership in making the gospel relevant to the many problems that arise as South Africa finds itself being reshaped.

Pretoria (South Africa), Richard A. Kraft, Bishop. PRAY for a government of national unity and the church's ministry of reconciliation; for the spread of spiritual renewal to undergird the growth of ministries; and for the planting of new congregations.

Friday *(Nativity of John the Baptist)*—**Saint Helena,** John Ruston, Bishop. GIVE THANKS for the generous support, in prayer and finance, from friends overseas. PRAY for the Lord's guidance in our endeavours to develop church youth groups, with the training of local youth leaders, and for a growing understanding of Christian stewardship.

Saint John's (South Africa), Jacob Z. Dlamini, Bishop.

Saint Mark the Evangelist (South Africa), Philip Le Feuvre, Bishop. PRAY for greater liberty in congregational worship, boldness in evangelism, and growth in holiness; and for an obedient understanding of our Lord's teaching about possessions and giving. PRAISE GOD for a balancing of the diocesan budget—with none to spare; and for development in active youth ministry, particularly for the Diocesan Youth Year Programme. (Have you any young people who would like to give a year of their lives in 1995?)

Order of Ethiopia, Sigqibo Dwane, Bishop.

Saturday: South Eastern Transvaal (South Africa), David Beetge, Bishop. PRAY for the Diocesan Development Trust launched in 1993; for vocations to the ordained ministry; and for our work amongst young people. GIVE THANKS for the Diocesan Renew programme; and for the development of lay ministries.

Swaziland , Lawrence Bekisisa Zulu, Bishop. PRAY for greater team work among the clergy and laity; for serious training of leaders to enable teaching in congregations at all levels; for a willingness to get involved in evangelising; and for our three religious houses and the means to expand Thokoza Church Centre.

Umzimvubu (South Africa), Geoffrey Davies, Bishop. GIVE THANKS for this, the newest diocese in the Province of Southern Africa. PRAY that the church may be a means of bringing people of diverse cultures, languages and races together, that, as they seek to establish a new South Africa, they may overcome the structural inequalities left by apartheid as well as the severe recession, drought and violence; for the Christian Training Centre for Human Development and Reconciliation; and for the growth of the Diocesan Endowment Fund.

Zululand (South Africa), Peter Harker, Bishop. GIVE THANKS for the election of our new Bishop. PRAY for God's blessing on the Bishop's ministry; for peace, justice and reconciliation; for a deepening of spirituality; and for an increasing awareness to accept full financial responsibility for the work of the diocese.

> *My God,*
> *I pray that I may so know you and love you*
> *that I may rejoice in you.*
> *And if I may not do so fully in this life*
> *let me go steadily on*
> *to the day when I come to that fullness....*
> *Let me receive*
> *That which you promised through your truth,*
> *that my joy may be full.*
>
> (St. Anselm)

Church of the Province of Southern Africa

1. CAPE TOWN
   • Cape Town
2. BLOEMFONTEIN
   • Bloemfontein
3. GEORGE
   • George
4. GRAHAMSTOWN
   • Grahamstown
5. KIMBERLEY and KURUMAN
   • Kimberley
6. LEBOMBO
   • Maputo
7. LESOTHO
   • Maseru
8. NATAL
   • Pietermaritzburg
9. NAMIBIA
   • Windhoek
10. NIASSA
    • Messumba
11. PORT ELIZABETH
    • Port Elizabeth
12. ST. HELENA
    • Jamestown
13. ST JOHN'S
    • Umtata
14. UMZIMVUBU
    • Kokstad
15. ST. MARK THE EVANGELIST
    • Pietersburg
16. SWAZILAND
    • Mbabane
17. ZULULAND
    • Eshowe
18. JOHANNESBURG
    • Johannesburg
19. KLERKSDORP
    • Klerksdorp
20. CHRIST THE KING
    • Sebokeng/Sharpeville
21. SOUTHEAST TRANSVAAL
    • Springs
22. PRETORIA
    • Pretoria

LEGEND

— National Borders
— Diocesan Borders
• See Cities

69

PRAY for the Church of the Province of Tanzania (Kanisa la Jimbo la Tanzania), John A. Ramadhani, Archbishop, with its 16 dioceses.

Archbishop John Ramadhani, who has announced his intention to retire as Primate, has presided during a period of rapid ecclesiastical growth despite an upsurge of Islamic Fundamentalism which threatens the foundations of our peaceful, cultural and inter-faith co-existence. He has also been leader at a transitional period of rapid social, political and economic changes in our society. Archbishop John is an exceptionally compassionate and careful listener. He has a big heart for the concerns of his people and his wise leadership strengths are built on this foundation.

Tanzania is now a multi-party democracy! Thanks be to God for the peaceful transition from a single party democracy to present. The role of the church in Tanzania is total involvement and commitment in sustaining the peace process.

PRAY for the Province as it goes through a transitional period with the retirement of the Archbishop.

Monday: Central Tanganyika, Mdimi Mhogolo, Bishop. Continue to PRAY for evangelism in the Kondoa area to the north of the diocese; for Christian education; for Msalato Bible College; for external Bible courses for lay readers, evangelists, catechists, Sunday school teachers, youth and women leaders, pastors and interested Christians; and for the pension scheme for 1,500 catechists.

Dar es Salaam, Basil M. Sambano, Bishop. PRAY that people of different cultural backgrounds in this multi-racial cosmopolitan city may always maintain real Christian love, hope, and a sense of oneness in one Lord—Jesus Christ; and that the increasing number of Christians may be reached by evangelism, good transport, literature and clergy housing facilities.

Kagera, Christopher Ruhuza, Bishop.

Tuesday: Mara, Gershom O. Nyaronga, Bishop.

Ruaha, Donald Mtetemela, Bishop. PRAISE GOD for the 84

Evangelists trained at our Lay Training Centre last year; and for the work of Evangelism Outreach already started in the west part of the diocese. PRAY for funds for these projects and for training of ordinands at St. Philip's Theological College; and that more people will be called to the ordained ministry.

Masasi, Christopher Bartholomew Sadiki, Bishop.

Wednesday *(St. Peter and St. Paul)*—**PRAY for the Anglican Centre in Rome and for Pope John Paul II.**

Morogoro, Dudley Mageni, Bishop. PRAY for our seminar for Pastors and their wives that is to take place from the 20th to 30th September; and that the Lord may give us the funds needed.

Mount Kilimanjaro, Simon Makundi, Bishop.

Mpwapwa, Simon Chiwanga, Bishop. PRAY for primary evangelism in Kibakwe and Chinyika deaneries; for the Training in Discipleship program; and for the stewardship program. THANK GOD for the completion of the Diocesan Cathedral Church, consecrated to All Saints.

Thursday: **Rift Valley,** Alpha Mohamed, Bishop.

Ruvuma, Stanford S. Shauri, Bishop.

South West Tanganyika, Charles J. Mwaigo, Bishop. GIVE THANKS for the rapid growth of the church in areas of primary evangelism. PRAY for the parishes as they actively now engage in Christian stewardship; and for the plans to divide the diocese in a few years' time.

Tabora, Francis Ntiruka, Bishop. PRAY for plans for building a Training Centre for the diocese; for more pastors and evangelists; and for Evangelism Outreach in new areas in the North of the diocese.

Friday *(Ganada Day)*—**PRAY for Canada.**

The Anglican Church of Canada presently is celebrating the centennial of the creation of General Synod which, in 1893, formed a national church out of what had been several regional bodies. During a three-year period we are remembering who we are, and seeking to discern the future of our mission and ministry.

A milestone for us was a special centennial service held last September, in which every diocese was linked by audio connection. Looking ahead, we have undertaken a programme of strategic planning that will give us a map to guide us into new ways of being the church. As part of that process, Canadian Partners in Mission and a national Ministry Symposium in 1993 will help provide insight and direction.

Aboriginal peoples of Canada continue to struggle to have their hopes realized. As a church, we are engaged in the follow-up of two significant events: the second national Native Convocation held last summer, and the report of the Residential Schools Task Force. This last has explored the pain experienced by many people of the First Nations who saw traditional values, education and culture severely affected by European standards and institutions. We continue to wrestle with how best we can support and strengthen the aspirations and endeavours of aboriginal peoples.

PRAY for the Primate of Canada, Archbishop Michael Peers; for the staff of Church House in Toronto. PRAY for those engaged as partners in world mission and those engaged as partners in Canadian mission; and for the Anglican contribution to work done ecumenically addressing the concerns of refugees, aid to developing countries, and aboriginal issues.

Saturday: Victoria Nyanza (Tanzania), John Changee, Bishop.

Western Tanganyika (Tanzania), Gerald Mpango, Bishop.

Zanzibar and Tanga (Tanzania), Archbishop John Ramadhani, Bishop. PRAY for integrity and right priorities in our drive towards self reliance and growth; that we may be made more aware of our spiritual and social responsibilities and, by the grace of God, be given the strength and resources to meet them; and for those who are especially entrusted to work among youth and in mother and child care.

Make us remember, O God, that every day is your gift, to be used according to your command.

(Samuel Johnson)

Province of Tanzania

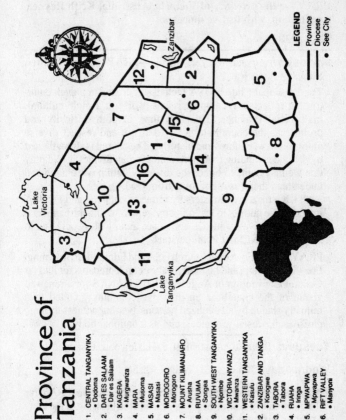

LEGEND

─── Province
─── Diocese
● See City

1. CENTRAL TANGANYIKA
   ● Dodoma
2. DAR ES SALAAM
   ● Dar es Salaam
3. KAGERA
   ● Murgwanza
4. MARA
   ● Musoma
5. MASASI
   ● Masasi
6. MOROGORO
   ● Morogoro
7. MOUNT KILIMANJARO
   ● Arusha
8. RUVUMA
   ● Songea
9. SOUTH WEST TANGANYIKA
   ● Njombe
10. VICTORIA NYANZA
    ● Mwanza
11. WESTERN TANGANYIKA
    ● Kasulu
12. ZANZIBAR AND TANGA
    ● Korogwe
13. TABORA
    ● Tabora
14. RUAHA
    ● Iringa
15. MPWAPWA
    ● Mpwapwa
16. RIFT VALLEY
    ● Manyoni

PRAY for the province of Victoria, Australia, Keith Rayner, Archbishop, with its five dioceses.

Map, p. 30.

Monday *(Independence Day, USA)***—PRAY for the United States of America.**

The Episcopal Church USA includes churches in eleven countries. It reflects the complex issues of life in a multi-cultural, multi-racial Province. This is a time of both difficulty and promise as the church struggles to affirm and respect diverse points of view, cultures and histories. The church is strengthened by the understanding that more unites it than divides it. We pray that we may come to honor the diversity within our church and understand that it is a gift to us from God.

All Christians are ministers by virtue of baptism, and ECUSA intends to be faithful to that ministry, remembering the baptismal promise to strive for justice and peace among all people and to seek and serve Christ in all persons.

PRAY for The Episcopal Church USA and Edmond L. Browning, Presiding Bishop, and his staff, as the church prepares for its 71st General Convention in August. GIVE THANKS for a renewed vision of the church as an inclusive community called to a ministry shared by all baptized persons, bearing witness through parishes, dioceses, provinces, and as a national body.

Tuesday: Ballarat (Australia), J. Hazlewood, Bishop.

Wednesday: Bendigo, B. Wright, Bishop.

Thursday: Gippsland, Colin D. Sheumack, Bishop. PRAY for the election of a new bishop this year and the blessing of the Holy Spirit on his ministry.

Friday: Melbourne, Archbishop Keith Rayner, Bishop; John Stewart, John Bayton, John Wilson, James Grant, Assistant Bishops. PRAY for a quickening of church life in the 240 parishes of the diocese, for deepened fellowship, and an enhanced capacity to reach out to the community with the gospel; and for church welfare agencies, especially their care for children and families in poverty. GIVE THANKS for the ministry of women, and openness to their gifts and insights.

Saturday: **Wangaratta,** Robert G. Beal, Bishop. GIVE THANKS for the ministry of the laity of the diocese. PRAY for the development of outreach in the growing areas of Albury/Wodonga; and for the process of the election of a new bishop.

O God, we do not desire new contentions and discord. We pray only that the Son of God, our Lord Jesus Christ, who for us died and rose from the grave, will guide us, that all who are in many churches and many communions may be one Church, one Communion and one in him. As he himself earnestly prayed for us in his hour of death, saying, "I pray also for those who through your Word will believe in me, that they may be one as you, Father are in union with me and I with you, and that they may be one in us," so also we pray. Amen.
(Philip Melanchthon)

PRAY for the Church of Pakistan, Zahir-ud-din Mirza, Moderator, with its eight dioceses.

The Church of Pakistan was formed in 1970 as a union of four churches: The Church of Pakistan (Anglican), the United Church of North India and Pakistan (Presbyterian), the United Methodist Church (American Methodist) and the Lutheran Church of Pakistan.

Map, p. 60.

(Sea Sunday)—**PRAY for the work of missions to seamen throughout the world.**

Monday: Faisalabad, Moderator Zahir-ud-din Mirza, Bishop.
  Hyderabad, Bashir Jiwan, Bishop.

Tuesday: Karachi, Arne Rudvin, Bishop.

Wednesday: Lahore, Dr. Alexander J. Malik, Bishop.

Thursday: Multan, Samuel D. Chand, Bishop.

Friday: Peshawar, S.L. Alexander, Bishop.

Saturday: Raiwind, Samuel Azariah, Bishop.
  Sialkot, Samuel Parvaiz, Bishop.

> *O Creator and Mighty God,*
> *you have promised*
> *strength for the weak*
> *rest for the labourers*
> *light for the way*
> *grace for the trials*
> *help from above*
> *unfailing sympathy*
> *undying love.*
> *O Creator and Mighty God*
> *help us to continue in your promise. Amen.*
>   (Prayer from Pakistan)

PRAY for the province of Ontario, Canada, John A. Baycroft, Archbishop, with its seven dioceses.

GIVE THANKS for more than 300,000 committed Christians in parishes ranging from Canada's largest metropolitan centre to small, isolated northern villages. PRAY for insight, courage and sensitivity in our witness within an increasingly multi-faith society.

Map, p. 33.

Monday: Algoma, L.E. Peterson, Bishop. PRAY that every baptized person will fulfill their ministry and mission as Jesus calls and directs them; and that the leadership of the churches encourage and support these ministries.

Tuesday: Huron, Percy O'Driscoll, Bishop; C. Robert Townshend and Jack P. Peck, Suffragans. PRAY for the clergy and people of the diocese as we continue to encourage people to live up to the baptismal covenant and search for ways to mark the Decade of Evangelism.

Wednesday: Moosonee, Caleb J. Lawrence, Bishop. GIVE THANKS for evangelism initiatives as part of the mission of the whole church. PRAY for all engaged in our CTEE Christian Leadership Formation Programme; and for setting up a companion relationship with the Diocese of Paraguay.

Thursday: Niagara, Walter G. Asbil, Bishop. To implement the Futures Task Force Report, "Making the Change," the diocese has been re-organized into six Regions and three Divisions of Ministry. PRAY for new Archdeacons and Regional Deans, and for clergy and laity on Regional Councils and Divisions of Ministry. GIVE THANKS for the dedication of many people who work for the strengthening and outreach of the church; and for the Youth Ministry and Seniors' Ministry in many parishes and regions of the diocese.

Friday *(St. Mary Magdalene)*—**Ontario,** Peter Mason, Bishop. PRAY for a developing sense of evangelism and outreach; for victims of sexual abuse and their families; and for the work of long range planning.

Ottawa, Archbishop John A. Baycroft, Bishop; Russell Hatton, Bishop Ordinary to the Forces. PRAY for the diocese as it adjusts to the sudden deaths of Archbishop Lackey and Assistant Bishop Goodings; for grace and guidance for the new Diocesan Bishop and for the empowerment of the ministries of the whole people of God; and for a continuing growth in confidence in the church's role in actualizing the gospel in contemporary culture.

Saturday: Toronto, Terence Finlay, Bishop; Arthur D. Brown, Joachim Fricker, Taylor Pryce and Douglas Blackwell, Area Bishops. GIVE THANKS for our commitment to build growing, caring communities emphasizing spirituality, evangelism and social justice. PRAY that we may be equipped to grapple with the issues of the 90s with sensitivity, compassion and justice.

Welcome
You have come from afar
and waited long and are wearied:
Let us sit side by side
sharing the same bread drawn from the same source
to quiet the same hunger that makes us weak.
Then standing together
let us share the same spirit, the same thoughts
that once again draw us together in friendship and unity and peace.

(Pières d'Ozawamick, Canadian Indian)

PRAY for the Scottish Episcopal Church, Richard Holloway, Primus, with its seven dioceses.

The most significant political challenge that faces the people of the United Kingdom is their relationship to the new Europe. The emergence of a new European consciousness offers new possibilities to the churches of Europe and we pray that Christians will unite in an endeavour, in Jacques Delors' words, "to be the soul of Europe."

The new European consciousness, with its emphasis on de-volved power, is of particular importance to the small nations of Europe, like Scotland, who often feel pushed to the political margins by their own governments.

PRAY for the Scottish churches as they struggle to be faithful to the Holy Spirit in meeting these new challenges; PRAY that the Holy Spirit will kindle a flame of courage and faith among the people of the Scottish churches that they may rise to the challenge of a new era. GIVE THANKS for many investments released in new mission; for three new Bishops; for the theological college becoming a lay and clergy training institute. PRAY for the church as it debates divisive issues of women and the priesthood.

Monday *(St. James)*—**Aberdeen and Orkney,** Andrew Bruce Cameron, Bishop. PRAY for the diverse challenges of the church's mission in city, rural and island situations within this diocese; for the development of our training in ministry programme; and for our response to new opportunities in mis-sion.

Tuesday: **Argyll and The Isles,** Douglas Cameron, Bishop. PRAY for us in this large and sparsely populated diocese; for the ministry of Bishop's House, Iona; for the Retreat Centre on the Isle of Cumbrae; and for the work of the Mission and Stewardship committees.

Wednesday: **Brechin,** Robert T. Halliday, Bishop. GIVE THANKS for the work of the Poverty Action Team in Brechin, and for the building of a shared hall in Portlethen giving a new

Episcopalian centre there. PRAY for the developments, provincial and diocesan, in training stipendiary and non-stipendiary clergy; and for the calling of a religious order to work in the housing area of Kirkton in Dundee.

Thursday: Edinburgh, Richard Holloway, Bishop and Primus; Patrick Rodger, Assistant. PRAY for a renewed vision for growth and mission in congregations during the Decade of Evangelism; and for unity within the Province and across the Christian traditions in Scotland. GIVE THANKS for new movements in spirituality.

Friday: Glasgow and Galloway, John M. Taylor, Bishop. GIVE THANKS for the new Diocesan Strategy. PRAY for Million for Mission projects in deprived city areas: for Mission Audit and Stewardship initiatives in all charges: and for "Kindleflame" to encourage evangelism.

Moray, George M. Sessford, Bishop.

Saturday: St. Andrews, Dunkeid and Dunblane, Michael Geoffrey Hare Duke, Bishop. PRAY for the diocese in its preparation to elect a successor to Bishop Michael when he retires after 25 years in October.

Lord God, we thank you
For calling us into the company
Of those who trust in Christ
And seek to obey his will.
May your Spirit guide and strengthen us
In mission and service to your world;
For we are strangers no longer
But pilgrims together on the way to your kingdom. Amen.
(Jamie Wallace)

The Scottish Episcopal Church

1. MORAY ROSS and CAITHNESS
   • Inverness
2. ABERDEEN and ORKNEY
   • Aberdeen
3. BRECHIN
   • Dundee
4. ST. ANDREWS DUNBLANE
   and DUNKELD
   • Perth
5. ARGYLL and THE ISLES
   • Oban
6. EDINBURGH
   • Edinburgh
7. GLASGOW and GALLOWAY
   • Glasgow

LEGEND
— Province
= Diocese
• See City

The Church in Wales

1. BANGOR
   • Bangor
2. ST. ASAPH
   • St. Asaph
3. ST. DAVIDS
   • St. Davids
4. SWANSEA and BRECON
   • Brecon
5. LLANDAFF
   • Cardiff
6. MONMOUTH
   • Newport

PRAY for the province of British Columbia and the Yukon, Canada, Douglas Hambidge, Archbishop, with its six dioceses.

The province covers the whole of the civil province of British Columbia and Yukon Territory. During the past years the dioceses have worked to encourage the life of the province in co-operative ventures such as a conference on "The Small Church," and the vocational diaconate. The dioceses work through the Standing Committees of the province—Social Concerns, Ministry and Parish and Diocesan Concerns.

PRAY for the province as it prepares to support a newly elected Metropolitan.

Map, p. 33.

Monday: British Columbia, R. Barry Jenks, Bishop.

Tuesday: Caledonia, John E. Hannen, Bishop. PRAY for the diocese as we seek to enter into a process of planning for our future in a way which enables us to fulfil more effectively the mission and ministry which God has entrusted to us.

Wednesday: Cariboo, James D. Cruickshank, Bishop. PRAY for the Healing Ministry particularly around First Nation communities; for children participating in the Life in the Eucharist Programme; for stewardship development; for openness to change. GIVE THANKS for the baptismal ministry of all of the people of Cariboo, ordained and laity.

Thursday: Kootenay, David P. Crawley, Bishop. GIVE THANKS for the devotion and commitment of our laity and clergy. PRAY for shared ministries; for the development of Baptismal Ministry; that all may work for reconciliation in a broken world; and for justice and equity.

Friday: New Westminster, Bishop to be elected. PRAY for the congregations of the diocese as the gospel is proclaimed in a multicultural and affluent society; and for wisdom and insight in the proper use of property and personnel.

Saturday *(The Transfiguration)*—**Yukon,** R.C. Ferris, Bishop. GIVE THANKS for the life, witness and ministry of our small congregations. PRAY for a just culmination of many years of work by Indian leaders and governments for the Yukon Comprehensive Land Claims Settlement.

Lord God almighty,
I pray you for your great mercy and by the token of the
*   Holy Cross,*
Guide me to your will, to my soul's need, better than I can
*   myself;*
And shield me against my foes, seen and unseen;
And teach me to do your will
*   that I may inwardly love you before all things with a clean mind*
*   and a clean body.*
For you are my maker and my redeemer,
*   my help, my comfort, my trust, and my hope.*
Praise and glory be to you, now, ever and ever, world without end.

(Alfred the Great)

Province of Kenya

1. ELDORET
   • Eldoret
2. MASENO NORTH
   • Kakamega
3. MASENO WEST
   • Siaya
4. MASENO SOUTH
   • Kisumu
5. NAKURU
   • Nakuru
6. MT. KENYA CENTRAL
   • Muranga
7. MT. KENYA SOUTH
   • Kiambu
8. NAIROBI
   • Nairobi
9. KIRINYAGA
   • Kutus
10. MACHAKOS
    • Machakos
11. MOMBASA
    • Mombasa
12. NAMBALE
    • Nambale
13. EMBU
    • Embu
14. KATAKWA
    • Katakwa

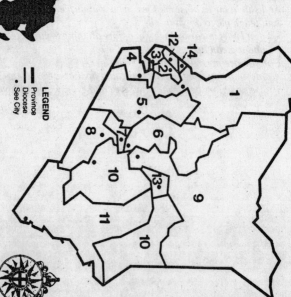

LEGEND
━━ Province
═ Diocese
• See City

PRAY for the Church of the Province of Kenya (Kanisa la Jimbo la Kenya), Manasses Kuria, Archbishop, with its 14 dioceses.

With a population of over 22,000,000 in a geographical area of 564,000 square miles, there are an estimated 1,500,000 Anglicans living in this Province. There are 453 parishes with over 500 clergy. Seven Bible colleges and one theological college prepare people for ministry. There are over 16,000,000 Christians with 26 percent being Roman Catholic and 17 percent part of African churches. Six percent of the population is Muslim.

Mombasa saw the arrival of Anglican missionaries in 1844. There was rapid growth and in 1885 the first Africans were ordained to the priesthood. As early as 1910 there was a mass movement of conversions in the country. In 1926 the Diocese of Mombasa was established. The first two Kenyan Bishops were consecrated in 1955. The church became part of the Province of East Africa, established in 1960, but by 1970 it was necessary to divide Kenya and Tanzania into separate Provinces.

Monday: Eldoret, Stephen Kewasis Nyorsok, Bishop. PRAY for Christians in the affected clash areas; for youth; for St. Mary's Guild; for the semi-arid areas in our diocese, Turkana and West Pokot; for our development staff as they move into regionalisation; and for reconciliation.

Katakwa, E. O. Okiring, Bishop.

Tuesday: Machakos, Benjamin Nzimbi, Bishop. THANK GOD for the training of clergy, evangelists and development workers in the diocese; and for construction of the Bishop's House. PRAY for the construction of the Lay Training and Development Centre; and that diocesan spiritual growth may deepen.

Maseno North, James I. Mundia, Bishop. THANK GOD that the subdivision of Butere and Munaaias has been effected as from 1st January, 1993. PRAY that men of God's choice be elected for these three dioceses.

Wednesday: Maseno South, J. H. Okullu, Bishop.

Maseno West, J. O. Wesonga, Bishop.

Thursday: Mombasa, C. D. Nzano, Bishop.

Mount Kenya Central, Bishop to be chosen..

Friday: Mount Kenya East (Kenya), Bishop to be chosen.

Mount Kenya South (Kenya), George M. Njuguna, Bishop. PRAY for Bishop Karwki Integrated Training Course to be able to organize many courses; for our Diocesan Industrial Training Centre to get enough finances for running courses for youth; and for the new bishop's house which is under construction. THANK GOD for many people getting saved through missions; and for the TEE Course.

Mount Kenya West (Kenya), Alfred Chipman, Bishop. GIVE THANKS for the creation of Mount Kenya West diocese from Mount Kenya Central in 1993; for retirement of Bishop John Mahiaini in November 1993; for the training of 20 girls in motor engineering and 50 girls trained by Mothers' Union for tailoring; for spiritual growth among youths. PRAY that God may bless the new Bishops of the subdivided dioceses; that projects like root crop, initiated at Karaha for human development by Bishop Mahiaini, may spread to all local congregations; and that God may provide a suitable Mothers' Union Chairlady after retirement of Mrs. Mahiaini (who has initiated projects like Girls Hostel and the Goat Project); that peace may prevail in our country during this era of multipartism.

Nairobi (Kenya), Archbishop Mannasses Kuria, Bishop.

Saturday: Nakuru (Kenya), Stephen Njihia Mwangi, Bishop. PRAY for our nation, that peace will prevail and injustice, falsehood and corruption be taken away.

Nambale (Kenya), I. Namango, Bishop.

O Saviour Christ, in whose way of love lies the secret of all life, and the hope of all men, we pray for quiet courage to match this hour. We did not choose to be born or to live in such an age; but let its problems challenge us, its discoveries exhilarate us, its injustices anger us, its possibilities inspire us, and its vigour renew us, for your kingdom's sake.

PRAY for the Anglican Church of Korea, Bishop Simon S. Kim, Archbishop, with its three dioceses.

Korea is a country of tensions and divisions. One millennium as a unified autonomous nation ended in 1910 when the Japanese took it as a colony. The World War II victors, who drove out the Japanese, divided the country for military convenience in 1945. Since then, the peoples' most fervent desire has been for reunification. The three-year fratricidal "Korean War" was an attempt on the part of the North to reunite the peninsula by force. Heavily armed, both sides still confront each other despite the forty-year-old armistice. The church makes it clear that it is the Province of the whole peninsula.

There is a clash between modernity and tradition, between a new urban industrialized society and an old rural agrarian one, between new demands for political participation and social justice and the old hierarchial, authoritarian order.

The twenty-five percent of the population in the south that is Christian is divided into one hundred fourteen denominations. This church, which has a vocation to strive for Christian unity, works and prays for the coming of the Kingdom, that all may enjoy unity, equality, justice and peace.

Monday (*St. Mary the Virgin*)—**Pusan (Korea),** Bundo C.H. Kim, Bishop. PRAY for the Decade of Evangelism and the accomplishment of the first five-year plan. GIVE THANKS for the establishment of the Bansong Outreach for the poor and pray for its development. PRAY for the setting up of new parishes in Kumi, Kimchon and Cheju Island.

Tuesday: Seoul (Korea), Archbishop Simon S. Kim, Bishop. GIVE THANKS for the inauguration of the Province and the installation of its first Primate. PRAY for the gathering of funds needed to upgrade buildings and faculty of the Anglican University; for North Korea and the reunion of North and South Korea; for the provision of churches in areas of new growth; and for the four Houses of Sharing and two Social Centers in the diocese.

Wednesday: Taejon (Korea), P. Hwan Yoon, Bishop.

Thursday: PRAY for the Anglican Family & Community Network.

Friday: PRAY for the Anglican Liturgical Network.

Saturday: PRAY for the Inter-Anglican Refugee Network.

Lord, with Korean Christians, we pray for the unification of their land, and the creation of a new, just and peaceful future. Amen.

Lord,
thanks to you
the dividing wall of the temple is no longer a problem for us,
but the separating walls which we continue to build
most certainly are.
So Lord,
whether we are in Soweto,
Belfast or on the 38th parallel,
or a member of an ordinary Christian congregation somewhere,
putting up all the barriers common to human communities
the world over,
show us how we may begin instead to take them down. Amen.

Lord, break down the walls that separate us
and unite us in a single body.

(Chorus of the theme song;
Fifth Assembly of the WCC, Nairobi)

PRAY for the Church of the Province of West Africa with its 11 dioceses.

The Province's beloved Archbishop George D. Browne died in 1993, having suffered for the faith and for his people in the terrible Liberian civil war.

Ghana has ended nearly twelve years of military rule. Although some parties boycotted the parliamentary elections to reintroduce constitutional government, the new democratic institutions should promote wider participation in public affairs. International confidence in the government should also increase and this should attract more external investment to promote the national development.

The church contributed to the programmes to educate the public and to prepare the way towards constitutional rule. However, the boycott of the parliamentary elections by some parties has called for increased prayer and intensive negotiation to ensure national unity and peace.

The church continues to grapple with the challenge to compose a liturgy which expresses the Good News within the Ghanaian cultural context, of which music and dance are characteristic.

GIVE THANKS as we enter the second year of constitutional rule in Ghana, for God's blessing and guidance. PRAY that the welfare of the people will increasingly receive attention; that we have vision and courage in our search for economic and health projects to alleviate suffering and to generate income to finance church projects and the needs of the church throughout the Province.

Monday: Accra (Ghana), Francis W. Thompson, Bishop. THANK GOD for his many blessings; for completion of rehabilitation work of Bishopscourt and offices; for the Cathedral Centenary celebrations; for new opportunities and for the work of the church in this diocese, and for continuing support from our parishes. PRAY for vision and courage, for understanding and deeper commitment and devotion of the clergy and laity to the mission of the church.

Bo (Sierra Leone), Michael Keili, Bishop.

Tuesday: Cape Coast (Ghana), Kobina Quashie, Bishop. THANK GOD for blessings received during our first year of the second episcopacy. PRAY for unity, caring and sharing attitudes in this diocese so that poorer parishes may not want, and richer ones learn to give generously.

Freetown (Sierra Leone), P.E.S. Thompson, Bishop. GIVE THANKS for the new awakening to political maturity in our country. PRAY that the awakening of God's Spirit in the church may grow stronger to make us equal to the tasks of witness.

Wednesday *(St. Bartholomew)*—**The Gambia,** S. Tilewa Johnson, Bishop. PRAY for diocesan unity, the work of the rural evangelists, and concrete progress with the centre for Christian Education and Development at Banjulnding. GIVE THANKS for renewed vitality and a sense of direction in the diocese after a period of uncertainty.

Thursday: Guinea, Prince E.S. Thompson, Acting Bishop. PRAY for vocations to holy orders.

Koforidua (Ghana), Robert G.A. Okine, Bishop. THANK GOD for the continuing manifestation of the gifts of the Holy Spirit in our ministry. PRAY for more financial assistance to enable us to honour our heavy commitments to the ministerial formation of our growing number of vocations.

Friday: Kumasi (Ghana), Edmund Yeboah, Bishop. GIVE THANKS with the people of Ghana for a peaceful transition from eleven years' military rule to a democratic government; for UTO financial assistance to build a home for the Diocesan Bishop; and for a successful 20th anniversary (in 1993) of the inauguration of the diocese.

Liberia, Bishop to be chosen. GIVE THANKS for the life and ministry of Archibshop George D. Browne. PRAY for peace in this country in which so many have been slaughtered in civil war.

Saturday: Sekondi (Ghana), Theophilus Annobil, Bishop. THANK GOD for his many blessings, protection and guidance. PRAY for effective diocesan planning for the clergy who work in the remote parts of the diocese; for effective evangelism; for our medical work in our clinics, especially the new clinic at Bamiaankor; and for our Vocational Training School.

Sunyani and Tamale (Ghana), Joseph K. Dadson, Bishop. GIVE THANKS for continued ministry—lay and ordained—in our vast challenging diocese; for the fourth republican government of Ghana; and for our establishment of Bishop Aglionby Memorial Endowment Fund for Mission Development. PRAY for plans to make Sunyani a separate diocese; for resources for our Mission Development programmes; for commitment to renewal and transformation; for the visit of Sharing of Ministries Abroad (SOMA) (UK) 1993 and their training programme; and for Ghana that government and people practice dialogue.

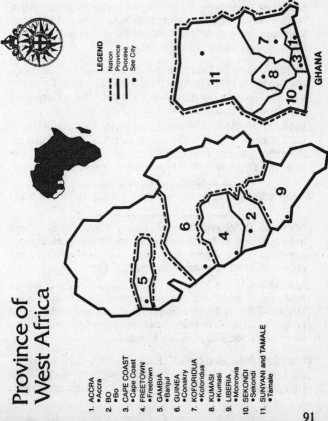

Province of West Africa

LEGEND
Nation
Province
Diocese
See City

GHANA

1. ACCRA
   • Accra
2. BO
   • Bo
3. CAPE COAST
   • Cape Coast
4. FREETOWN
   • Freetown
5. GAMBIA
   • Banjul
6. GUINEA
   • Conakry
7. KOFORIDUA
   • Koforidua
8. KUMASI
   • Kumasi
9. LIBERIA
   • Monrovia
10. SEKONDI
    • Sekondi
11. SUNYANI and TAMALE
    • Tamale

PRAY for the province of the Mid-west, USA, Bishop Roger White, President, with its 14 dioceses. (province V)

Map, pp. 22-23.

Monday: Chicago, Frank T. Griswold, Bishop.

Eau Claire, William C. Wantland, Bishop. PRAY for our expanding ministry to the Hmong and other Southeast Asian refugee people; and for continued healing between Indian and white communities. GIVE THANKS for continued growth and strength, including new congregations.

Tuesday: Fond du Lac, Bishop to be chosen. PRAY for small town and rural congregations; for renewal ministries; for ministry to the aging, the hungry and to Southeast Asian refugees; and for continuing fidelity and witness to the catholic faith.

Indianapolis, Edward W. Jones, Bishop. PRAY for us as host to the Episcopal Church's General Convention. PRAY also for those diocesan institutions which, in the name of Christ, offer hope to the homeless, the hungry, and the friendless.

Wednesday *(Malaysia Day)*—**PRAY for Malaysia.** (see p. 54)

Michigan, R. Steward Wood Jr., Bishop. PRAY for our efforts to address institutional racism, to prepare for the creation of two new dioceses out of the present one, to work among the poor and oppressed, and to become evangelists for Christ.

Milwaukee, Roger J. White, Bishop. GIVE THANKS for the continued development of new parishes; for our developing Hispanic Ministry; for the continued sharing of our catechumenate process with the whole church; and for our young people, as they move into leadership roles in the church.

Thursday: Missouri, Hays H. Rockwell, Bishop. PRAY for the strengthened presence of our church among the poor and for the strengthening and renewal of the priestly vocation in our diocese.

Northern Indiana, Francis C. Gray, Bishop. PRAY for a year long capital funds campaign, the results of which will allow us to open new congregations; for urban work in Northwest Indiana, and for youth ministry.

Friday: Northern Michigan, Thomas K. Ray, Bishop. PRAY for growth in understanding the vows of baptism, and support for use of spiritual gifts on a daily basis; for the unemployed and those affected by statewide decreases in social services; for the protection of this fragile environment, and its responsible use; and for all the reordering of our common life along baptismal lines.

Ohio, Bishop to be chosen. PRAY for the new Bishop and for Arthur B. Williams, Jr., Suffragan. GIVE THANKS for signs of renewed life in this 176th year of diocesan ministry.

Quincy, Bishop to be chosen; Br. John-Charles, FODC, Assisting Bishop. GIVE THANKS for a new mission, St. Andrew's, El Paso, and possible ministry in Eureka, Illinois.

Saturday: Southern Ohio, Herbert Thompson Jr., Bishop. PRAY for our newly-created Deaneries and their participation in outreach and mutual ministry; and for clergy and lay people as they seek to respond to the challenge of building the "New Jerusalem" through their witness to the poor and the oppressed. GIVE THANKS for the designation of Christ Church, Cincinnati, as the new Diocesan Cathedral.

Springfield, Peter H. Beckwith, Bishop. PRAY for the work of small churches; for new work; for the Decade of Evangelism; for a deepening spirituality and for faithfulness in stewardship; and that God will guide our work in these complex and difficult days.

Western Michigan, Edward L. Lee, Jr., Bishop. PRAY for the Year of Action, the third phase of the diocese's strategic planning program; and for the program Commissions: Stewardship, Evangelism and Missions, Worship, Christian Formation, Ministry within the Church, Ministry to the World, Youth Ministries, Campus Ministry, and Finance.

You have given so much to me,
Give one thing more, a grateful heart.
(George Herbert)

The Episcopal Church of the Sudan

1. KHARTOUM
   Khartoum
2. KADUGLI
   Kadugli
3. WAU
   Wau
4. RUMBEK
   Rumbek
5. BOR
   Bor
6. YAMBIO
   Yambio
7. MARIDI
   Maridi
8. MUNDRI
   Mundri
9. JUBA
   Juba
10. YEI
    Yei
11. KAJOKEJI
    Kajokeji

LEGEND

|| Province
| Diocese
• See City

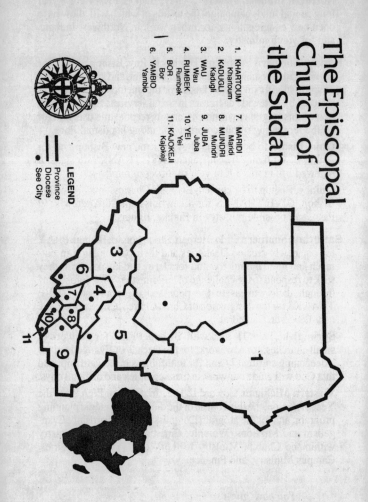

PRAY for the Episcopal Church of the Sudan, Benjamin W. Yugusuk, Archbishop, with its 11 dioceses.

In a country that is over 70 percent Muslim and 10 percent traditional religions, Anglicans and Roman Catholics make up the largest Christian population. The total population of the Sudan is over 28,000,000 in a vast geographical area of over 2,000,000 square miles. There are 400 clergy serving in 275 churches.

The Church Missionary Society (CMS) began work in 1899 in Omdurman, an area overwhelmingly Muslim. Christianity spread rapidly among black Africans of the Southern region. Until 1974 the Sudan was a single diocese under the jurisdiction of the Jerusalem Archbishopric. From that time there have been four dioceses, each under a Sudanese bishop, and the church gained its autonomy. Plagued with almost continual civil and religious strife between North and South and from a constant flow of refugees in and out of the country, the church has suffered much. In the midst of its suffering it has maintained a strong testimony to its faith.

PRAY for Benjamin Wani Yugusuk, Archbishop and Metropolitan; Daniel Zindo, Dean; and Nelson K. Nyumbe, Provincial Secretary; for the grace and peace of God to heal wounds of six years of crisis; for the whole Province to continue in the same spirit of re-union; for development of a proposed diocese; and for new Bishops in war-torn Sudan.

Monday: Bor, Nathaniel Garang, Bishop; Kedikia Mabior, Suffragan (*Malakal Area*); and Daniel Deng, Suffragan (*Renk Area*). PRAY that God will sustain a proposed diocese; and for pastoral care of Christians in refugee camps.

Juba, Archbishop Benjamin Wani Yugusuk, Bishop; Michael S. Lugor, Suffragan; Matia L. Rianga, Suffragan (*Rokon Area*); Wilson Arop, Suffragan (*Torit Area*). PRAY for our Bishops; for Juba Bible Training Institute; and for displaced and needy persons to be cared for with truth.

Tuesday: Kaduguli, Mubarak Khamis, Bishop; Peter El Birish, Suffragan (*Kacha Area*). PRAY for our Bishops; for God's protection; and for peace among Muslims, religious tolerance and understanding in Muslim dialogue.

Kajokeji, Manase B. Dawidi, Bishop. PRAY for grace and love among clergy ministering in refugee camps and among displaced persons in other areas; and for protection and cure of the Bishop's sickness.

Wednesday: Khartoum, Bulus Idris Tia, Bishop; Butrus Kowa Kori, Suffragan (*Portsudan Area*). PRAY for the spread of the gospel in the face of Islamization; for religious tolerance and understanding; and for the youth and Mothers' Union in the refugee camps.

Maridi, Joseph Marona, Bishop; Levi Hassan, Suffragan (*Ezo Area*). PRAY for refugees; and for development of youth and Mothers' Union work.

Thursday: Mundri, Eluzai G. Munda, Bishop; Ephraim Nathana, Suffragan (*Lui Area*). PRAY for pastoral care among displaced persons, with truth in God's mission; and for our training programme.

Rumbek, Gabriel Roric Jur, Bishop; Benjamin Mangar, Suffragan (*Yirol Area*). PRAY for those suffering because of the civil war; for displaced congregations in the camps; for peace in the Sudan; and for Rumbek's new Bible School, now based in Omdurman because of war in the South Sudan.

Friday: Wau, Henry Riak, Suffragan Bishop. PRAY for unity among Christians; for election of a Diocesan Bishop; and for youth and Mothers' Union work.

Saturday: Yambio, Daniel M. Zindo, Bishop; Benjamin Ruate, Suffragan (*Tambura Area*). PRAY for the displaced Bishops, clergy and laity; and for unity in the face of suffering.

Yei, Seme L. Solomona, Bishop. PRAY for courage and strength in the spread of the word of God among refugees and displaced persons; for the grace of God in the midst of suffering and war; and for the Theological Education by Extension programme and Diocesan Bible Training programme.

PRAY for the province of New South Wales, Australia, Harry Goodhew, Archbishop, with its seven dioceses.

The province is the most populous in Australia, and bears the continuing burden of having three large cities with high unemployment, where industry is yet to emerge from recession. Each of these cities is also having to deal with a significant diversification in ethnic mix. An increasing number of migrants now come from South East Asia. The church has a crucial role to play in relieving the most urgent effects of poverty through its welfare arm, encouraging communities to overcome racial and ethnic barriers and to live at peace.

The rest of the province is predominantly rural, a sector again facing the harsh economic realities of falling prices for primary produce. It is also shouldering the burden of long-term drought. Here, too, the church must maintain its prophetic voice to government and industry, and continue to display the compassion of Christ. Three dioceses—Canberra-Goulburn, Newcastle and Riverina—have new bishops. The Archbishop of Sydney has assumed his new role as Metropolitan. Two of his major tasks are the building of unity within his diocese and its maintaining positive relations with the wider Australian church.

Map, p. 28.

Monday: Armidale, Peter Chiswell, Bishop. PRAY for the development of an evangelistic outlook and confidence throughout the diocese; and for the beginning of using honorary deacons in a supplementary ministry.

Tuesday: Bathurst, Bruce Wilson, Bishop. GIVE THANKS for the large number of new ordination candidates in training. PRAY for ministry among indigenous people in remote parishes; and for the pastoral work with our clergy of Archdeacon Norman Kempson.

Wednesday: Canberra and Goulburn (Australia), George Browning, Bishop. PRAY for the diocese as it defines its future directions; for the development of an Anglican presence in the new areas of Canberra, and in the rural city of Wagga Wagga and the coastal town of Batemans Bay; and for vigorous growth in lay ministry.

Thursday: Grafton (Australia), Bruce A. Schultz, Bishop. PRAY for implementation of strategic goals that will enable the diocese to be a Christian community of believers proclaiming a contemporary Jesus Christ; and for goals which consistently meet the needs of members of our community and the unchurched through energised, responsive ministries of clergy and laity.

Friday *(Papua New Guinea Day)*—**PRAY for Papua New Guinea.**

Newcastle (Australia), Roger Herft, Bishop. PRAY for our ability to respond to the challenges presented by greatly increased populations in many parts of the diocese; for our theological College of St. John the Evangelist and its work in training for priestly and lay ministry. GIVE THANKS for the great faithfulness and loyalty of our lay people.

Saturday: Riverina (Australia), Bruce Clark Bishop. GIVE THANKS for the election of our new bishop, and PRAY for us as we look afresh at the opportunities for worship and service before us.

Sydney (Australia), Archbishop Harry Goodhew, Bishop; Regional Bishops Peter Watson *(Parramatta)* and Paul Barnett *(North Sydney)*. PRAY for appointment of two new regional bishops (Wollongong and South Sydney) and the newly appointed archbishop; that the diocese may exhibit true growth; and that each member may live as an obedient witness to the love of Christ.

This is your harvest, Lord. We pray you send forth laborers into your harvest. We are your flock, O Lord. We pray you raise up faithful shepherds under the guidance of your Spirit. It is your world, O Lord, created, redeemed, sustained by your love. Teach us to care for your world in caring for all your children; through him who is our Good News always, Jesus Christ.

PRAY for the province of Central America and Mexico, Episcopal Church USA, Bishop Neptali Larrea, President, with its 14 dioceses. (province IX)

Dioceses in this area, now part of the Episcopal Church USA, are planning for the eventual establishment of a Province.

Map, pp. 22-23.

Monday: Central Ecuador, Neptali Larrea-Moreno, Bishop.

Colombia, Bernardo Merino-Botero, Bishop.

Cuernavaca (Mexico), Jose G. Saucedo, Bishop.

Tuesday: Dominican Republic, Julio C. Holguin, Bishop. PRAY for the continued opening of new missions; for God's guidance in the process of achieving autonomy through stewardship and evangelism; and for those planning our 1997 centennial celebration. GIVE THANKS for renewed lives through the theological education program.

El Salvador, Martin Barahona, Bishop. PRAY for the reconciliation and for the reconstruction of a new country, which has been destroyed by a 12-year war; and for the organization and consolidation of the Episcopal Church of El Salvador.

Wednesday *(St. Matthew)*—**Guatemala,** Armando Guerra, Bishop. PRAY for continued growth of the church; for the consolidation of regional work; and for the success of the Joint Diocesan Pastoral Plan to be implemented in 1990-2000.

Honduras, Leo Frade, Bishop. GIVE THANKS for God's help during a financial crisis; for church growth; and for many vocations. PRAY for new churches being planted; for financial resources to continue and expand our work, both social and religious; for our new government recently elected; and for the improvement of human rights in our country.

Thursday: Litoral (Ecuador), Martiniano Garcia-Montial, Bishop.

Mexico, Sergio Carranza-Gomez, Bishop. PRAY for a broad understanding of evangelism and a deep commitment to stewardship.

Friday: Nicaragua, Sturdie W. Downs, Bishop. PRAY for social stability, peace and job opportunities.

Northern Mexico, German Martinez, Bishop.

Panama, James Hamilton Ottley, Bishop; Victor A. Scantlebury, Suffragan. PRAY for a renewed spirit of unity, light and hope in a country afflicted by social, political and economic injustice.

Saturday: Southeast Mexico, Claro Huerta Ramos, Bishop. PRAY for reaching our goals of expansion; for the guidance of persons with priestly vocation; for our program of theological training by extension; for the respect and dignity of human beings; and for peace and justice among all nations.

Western Mexico, Samuel Espinoza, Bishop.

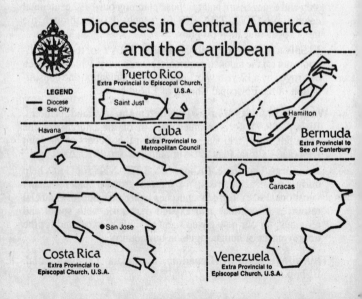

Dioceses in Central America and the Caribbean

LEGEND
— Diocese
• See City

Puerto Rico
Extra Provincial to Episcopal Church, U.S.A.
Saint Just

Cuba
Extra Provincial to Metropolitan Council
Havana

Bermuda
Extra Provincial to See of Canterbury
Hamilton

Costa Rica
Extra Provincial to Episcopal Church, U.S.A.
San Jose

Venezuela
Extra Provincial to Episcopal Church, U.S.A.
Caracas

PRAY for the Province of the West Indies, Orland U. Lindsay, Archbishop, with its eight dioceses.

This Province reaches into a scattered geographic area of 21 countries covering 106,244 square miles. There are 770,000 Anglicans with 892 churches and 368 clergy. The total population in these countries is 4,400,000, of which 4,100,000 are Christians.

The Church of England established missions in various West Indian territories that became British Colonies. In 1883 the Province was formed complete with a Primate and Synod.

Monday: **Barbados,** Drexel Gomez, Bishop.

Belize. Bishop to be chosen. PRAY for the Bishops of the Province of the West Indies as they deliberate over the selection of the bishop to succeed Brother Desmond, SSF, who died in August 1992.

Tuesday: **Guyana,** Randolph O. George, Bishop. GIVE THANKS for real prospects of change under democracy. PRAY for the church's mission to all the people of Guyana at this time of reconstruction.

Wednesday: **Jamaica,** Neville W. deSouza, Bishop.

Nassau and the Bahamas, Michael H. Eldon, Bishop. PRAY for the continued development of an inclusive diocesan stewardship programme; and for the formulation of a vision of mission. GIVE THANKS for the many expressions of support received as a result of Hurricane Andrew.

Thursday *(St. Michael and All Angels)*—**North Eastern Caribbean and Aruba,** Archbishop Orland Lindsay, Bishop; Alfred E. Jeffery, Suffragan. GIVE THANKS for the unity existing in this diocese of twelve islands. PRAY for the strengthening of the companion relationship with St. Albans and Southern Virginia; for more vocations to the ordained ministry; and for social outreach and Christian education programmes.

Friday: **Trinidad and Tobago,** Rawle E. Douglin, Bishop. PRAY for the nation as it struggles against the persistent debt and unemployment problems with the related social crises; and for the diocese under new episcopal leadership, that its mission and witness for Christ may be extended.

Saturday: **Windward Island,** Philip E.R. Elder, Bishop. PRAY for greater and deepening engagement of our people; for work with youth; for an increase of vocations; and for the parish of Holy Trinity, St. Vincent, as its parishioners grapple with the urgent problem of restoring their termite-ridden parish church and rectory.

O God, our Father,
the fountain of love, power and justice,
the God who cares,
particularly for the least,
the most suffering and the poorest among us.

O God, Lord of creation,
grant us today your guidance and wisdom
so that we may see the human predicament for what it is.

Give us courage and obedience
so that we may follow you completely.
Help us, Lord, to bear witness
to the cross of your son, our Lord Jesus Christ,
who alone is the reason for hope,
and in whose name we pray. Amen.

(Koson Srisang, Thailand)

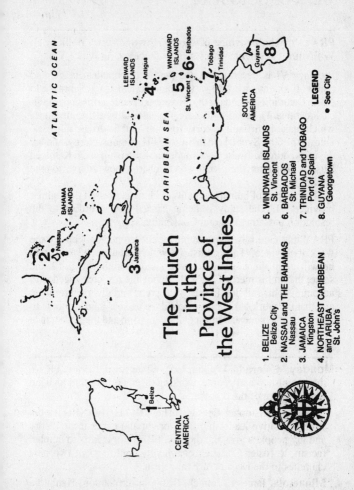

The Church
in the
Province of
the West Indies

1. BELIZE
   Belize City
2. NASSAU and THE BAHAMAS
   Nassau
3. JAMAICA
   Kingston
4. NORTHEAST CARIBBEAN
   and ARUBA
   St. John's

5. WINDWARD ISLANDS
   St. Vincent
6. BARBADOS
   St. Michael
7. TRINIDAD and TOBAGO
   Port of Spain
8. GUYANA
   Georgetown

ATLANTIC OCEAN

CARIBBEAN SEA

BAHAMA ISLANDS
Nassau

Jamaica

LEEWARD ISLANDS
Antigua

WINDWARD ISLANDS
St. Vincent · Barbados

Tobago
Trinidad

SOUTH AMERICA

Guyana

LEGEND
● See City

CENTRAL AMERICA
Belize

PRAY for the province of the Northwest, USA, William H. Wolfrum, President, with its eight dioceses. (province VI)

Province VI is described as the land of mountains, lakes, and plains. It extends from Iowa to Colorado and from Nebraska to North Dakota. The needs of the area are as diverse as the geographical locations. The conditions have presented unique circumstances which make it difficult to carry forward benefits to the dioceses. During the 60th Synod held in Sioux Falls, bishops, clergy, and lay deputies addressed these issues under the leadership of Dr. Kathleen Russell. Together the group was to chart a new course for the province.

The subject of human sexuality is being addressed throughout province VI. The study is being carried out according to the resolution passed at General Convention.

PRAY that God raise up committed, chosen people who see the work of province VI as a ministry to which he has called them; that he will grant them strength, power, and anointing to fulfill the same; that in his mercy God will provide the resources needed to accomplish his mission in this widespread and diverse province; and that the work of the province will be used as an instrument to glorify God's name and bring glory to his Son and the furtherance of his kingdom.

Map, pp. 22-23.

Monday: Colorado, William Jerry Winterrowd, Bishop. PRAY that the bishop and people, working together, may find a vision for the future of the diocese.

Iowa, C. Christopher Epting, Bishop. GIVE THANKS for the strong, positive leadership from bright and enthusiastic clergy and lay people across the diocese. PRAY for efforts to combat racism, to foster Christian community, and to plant two new churches in the Decade of Evangelism.

Minnesota, James L. Jelinek, Bishop-elect; Sanford Hampton, Suffragan. PRAY for our program of evangelism, development of new congregations, total ministry, education, and stewardship.

Tuesday: **Montana,** Charles I. (Ci) Jones, Bishop. PRAY for this large and sparsely populated diocese, that we may have faith that God is in charge and will lead us to new and exciting ways of doing ministry if we will have the courage to follow.

Wednesday: **Nebraska,** James E. Krotz, Bishop. GIVE THANKS for the successful "planting" of a new congregation in suburban Omaha. PRAY for our efforts to establish a second new congregation this year.

Thursday: **North Dakota,** Andrew Fairfield, Bishop. GIVE THANKS for renewed focus on development of this ministry of all the baptized. PRAY for congregational ministry leadership teams; for regional and diocesan education and support systems for ministry; and, during a time of continued drought on these Northern Plains, for rain.

Friday: **South Dakota,** Bishop to be chosen. PRAY for those who shall choose a bishop for this diocese, that we may receive a faithful pastor, who will care for God's people and equip us for our ministries.

Saturday: **Wyoming,** Bob Gordon Jones, Bishop. GIVE THANKS for standing in God's presence as his redeemed people. PRAY for those who do not yet believe and for those who have lost their faith, that the Spirit of God may bring the light of the gospel to them; and that the sacred life-giving story continues to be told in every land and in every tongue.

Lord, we thank you that our churches are like big families.
Lord, let your Spirit of reconciliation blow over all the earth.
Let Christians live your love.
Lord, we praise you with Europe's cathedrals,
with America's offerings
and with our African songs of praise.
Lord, we thank you that we have brothers in all the world.
Be with them that make peace.

(A prayer from West Africa.)

PRAY for the province of Rupert's Land, Canada, Walter Heath Jones, Archbishop, with its 10 dioceses.

Rupert's Land is a vast area covering 60 percent of the land mass of Canada. Isolation, loneliness, and travel of many, many miles are common.

PRAY for the Anglicans scattered from the Arctic to the Canada/USA border; and for the province as it works together in developing indigenous and new forms of ministry. GIVE THANKS for our real sense of unity and interdependence in this part of the church's body.

Map, p. 33.

Monday *(Thanksgiving Day, Canada)*: **The Arctic,** J. Christopher R. Williams, Bishop. PRAY for the new Suffragan Bishop, consecrated in August, 1993; and for the students of the Arthur Turner Training School, Pangnirtung, as they complete their course and are ordained this summer. GIVE THANKS to God for the continuing ministry of the lay leaders of our parishes and the growth in acceptance of responsibility by congregations.

Athabasca, John R. Clarke, Bishop. PRAY that the diocese will continue to focus on the need to be a church of mission and build the necessary bridges to communicate with the over 13,000 people who claim membership but are not involved in the life of the church.

Tuesday: Brandon, Malcolm Harding, Bishop. PRAY for the development and growth of our companion relationship with the Diocese of Southwest Tanganyika; for new forms of ministry in declining rural areas; for the ongoing work of the Diocesan Council of Indian and Metis Affairs; and for parish renewal, mission and ministry throughout the diocese.

Calgary, J. Barry Curtis, Bishop; Gary F. Woolsey, Assistant. PRAY for our continuing work to establish new parishes in growing areas and to revitilize existing congregations; for parishes, clergy and people in rural areas struggling to cope with severe difficulties in the agricultural economy; for the growth of the Logos Programme; and for Explorations in Ministry, an initiative to strengthen the ministry of lay leaders.

Wednesday: Edmonton, Kenneth L. Genge, Bishop. GIVE THANKS for "Opportunity 2000" Church Development Trust; for EFM (Education for Ministry) study program for laity; for increasing emphasis on preparation for baptism; and for Cursillo and renewed Christian life-style. PRAY for the generosity of friendship in response to Christ's call in John 15.

Keewatin, Thomas Collings, Bishop. PRAY for the new Suffragan Bishop with responsibility for Native Ministry (primarily in Northern Ontario). This completes the structure for an indigenous church there. GIVE THANKS for many bi-vocational priests, strong Native leadership and a vision of total ministry. PRAY for ministry training programs, cross-cultural ministry, families suffering from violence, and for the youth.

Thursday: Qu'Appelle, Eric Bays, Bishop. GIVE THANKS for growing ministry development in parishes and members' daily lives. PRAY for a developing partnership between parish and diocese in the carrying out of the church's mission in each community.

Rupert's Land, Archbishop Walter Heath Jones, Bishop. PRAY for growing unity in the diocese; for the strengthening of both lay and ordained ministry through the continuing education programs of St. John's College; for growth in rural and native parishes; and for the faithfulness and outreach of all our people.

Friday: Saskatchewan, Thomas O. Morgan, Bishop; Charles Arthurson, Suffragan (Native bishop among the Cree Indians). PRAY for ministry in scattered rural communities; for the training of Christian leaders and pastoral oversight for our Native Indian congregations; and for the strengthening of our sense of mission and outreach.

Saturday: Saskatoon, R. A. Wood, Bishop. GIVE THANKS for continuing support from all our people in these worrying times, and PRAY for our obedience to the guiding of the Holy Spirit as we begin a new chapter in the history of the diocese, looking for a fresh sense of direction, seeking to be the people of God in an ever-changing world.

PRAY for the province of New England, USA, Bishop Arthur Walmsley, President, with its seven dioceses. (province I)

Map, pp. 22-23.

Monday: **Connecticut,** Clarence Coleridge, Bishop; Jeffery Rowthorn, Suffragan. GIVE THANKS for the successful first year of All Saints Conference Center; for L'Eglise de l'Epiphanie, our first Haitian mission; and for the ministry of all our choirs and church musicians. PRAY for our newly elected Bishop; for a renewed resolve to address the issues of racism in our state and diocese; for the unemployed; and for the creation of new job opportunities throughout the state.

Maine, Edward C. Chalfont, Bishop.

Tuesday *(St. Luke)*—**Massachusetts,** David E. Johnson, Bishop; Barbara C. Harris, Suffragan. PRAY for a deepening commitment to one another as sisters and brothers in Christ as we evaluate the life, ministry and mission of the diocese; and for the guidance of the Holy Spirit as we seek new episcopal leadership.

Wednesday: **New Hampshire,** Douglas E. Theuner, Bishop. PRAY for good stewardship of our natural and human resources; and for the guidance of the Holy Spirit in the life of our congregations and our church-related schools: St. Paul's, Holderness, and White Mountain.

Thursday: **Rhode Island,** George N. Hunt, Bishop. PRAY for clarity of vision and the grace and courage to become what our vision calls us to be and to do as the body of Christ.

Friday: **Vermont,** Mary Adelia McLeod, Bishop-elect.

Saturday: **Western Massachusetts,** Robert S. Denig, Bishop. GIVE THANKS for a deepening commitment to prayer, community life, and mission within the diocese. PRAY for expanding ministries among Hispanics and others on the margins of our cities and towns.

PRAY for the Province of the Church in Wales (Eglwys yng Nghymru), Alwin R. Jones, Primate, with its six dioceses.

The history of Christianity in Wales goes back at least to the fourth century AD, but the Church in Wales came into existence as a separate Anglican Province only in 1920, when an Act of Parliament removed the four ancient dioceses of Bangor, St. Asaph, St. Davids and Llandaff from the jurisdiction of Canterbury, and ended their legal ties with the British state.

The Church in Wales is now one of the largest religious bodies in Wales and, since the severance of the state link in 1920 has come to be increasingly identified with the culture and aspirations of the communities of Wales. It is committed to a bilingual policy in its publications, worship and public affairs, and maintains a strong presence in educational institutions in the country. At present, it faces major social problems in the form of depopulation and the breaking up of communities in the rural areas, and long-term unemployment and privation in the former industrial heartlands of the south. In recent years, it has strengthened its commitment to community development work in deprived regions, to co-operation with other Christian bodies in Wales, by means of a covenant with several other denominations, and to evangelism and outreach to young people. Having begun early with the process of liturgical renewal, it continues this task with energy and resourcefulness. International links have always been particularly important, and strong contacts are maintained in Africa and the Caribbean in particular.

GIVE THANKS for renewed commitment to the church's partnership with the Children's Society in community development; and for new ideas and visions for rural ministry. PRAY for the unemployed and all whose jobs are under threat, in industry and countryside; and for the new proposals to improve the status of the Welsh language in law and public life.

Map, p. 81.

Monday *(St. James of Jerusalem)*—**Bangor,** Barry Morgan, Bishop. PRAY that we may be open to change in patterns of ministry and service; and for our response to the problems of our rural communities; and that whatever the decision about the ordination of women to the priesthood we may continue to work together in mutual love and trust.

Tuesday *(United Nations Day)* **—PRAY for world peace.**

Llandaff, Roy Thomas Davies, Bishop. THANK GOD for the response to the Decade of Evangelism within the diocese. PRAY for the strategy adopted to promote evangelism in our parishes.

Wednesday: Monmouth, Rowan Williams, Bishop. PRAY for further development in our commitment to evangelism and stewardship; and for vocations to lay and ordained ministry. GIVE THANKS for the continuing generosity of our people in community development work in depressed areas.

Thursday: Saint Asaph, Archbishop Alwyn Rice Jones, Bishop. PRAY for the new Assistant Bishop, D. Huw Jones, that together we may enable the whole diocese as a family to respond and participate in God's mission and ministry here.

Friday: St. David's, J. Ivor Rees, Bishop. THANK GOD for the work of the Council for Social Responsibility and all its outreach in deprived urban areas. PRAY for lasting solutions to the problems of rising unemployment in those areas and to the various problems affecting the life of our farming communities. PRAY with St. David that we shall "be joyful and keep our faith and trust."

Saturday: Swansea and Brecon, Dewi Morris Bridges, Bishop. PRAY for the unity in the life of the diocese and among the churches; and for the Brecon Cathedral Appeal and the development of the Cathedral's resources for worship, witness and welcome.

PRAY for the province of the Southwest, USA, Bishop Sam Hulsey, President, with its 12 dioceses. (province VII)

There is tremendous change across our province with new opportunities for ministry, especially with minority groups. We want to enable the work done at the Seminary of the Southwest in Austin and especially the Center for Hispanic Ministry located there. Province VII is interested in how the province structure can work better in the future church. We want to celebrate the tremendous diversity in the province and work to relate well with the church beyond our boundaries.

PRAY for God's blessing upon the mission of the church around this province; for mutual support of one another; and the concern of the Province VII Board to enable ministries of outreach and nurture within and beyond our borders.

Map, pp. 22-23.

Monday: **Arkansas,** Bishop to be chosen. PRAY for the new Bishop of the diocese; for clergy and lay leaders as they seek to support that episcopate; and for the continued companion relationship with the Diocese of South Dakota as they also welcome a newly elected diocesan.

    Dallas, James M. Stanton, Bishop. PRAY for the unity of our diocese as our new bishop assumes his duties. PRAY as well for the growth of the diocese as we seek to lift up Christ in our communities, parishes and missions.

Tuesday *(All Saints' Day)*—**Fort Worth,** Clarence C. Pope, Jr., Bishop; Jack Iker, Coadjutor.

    Kansas, William Edward Smalley, Bishop. PRAY for us as we seek to be the people of God in this new time of mission, primarily through spiritual development, stewardship, and new forms of ministry which honor and enable the ministry of all baptized persons.

Wednesday: **Northwest Texas,** Sam B. Hulsey, Bishop. PRAY for the new diocesan mission strategy, new forms of ministry, outreach to a growing minority population, the ministry of the Quarterman Conference Center, and the unity of the church.

Oklahoma, Robert M. Moody, Bishop.

Thursday: Rio Grande, Terence Kelshaw, Bishop. PRAISE GOD for continuing growth and mission; for the ministry of the four area deans and the full complement of clergy; for the immense ministry of church members in every walk of life; and for the efficient leadership of the Diocesan Councils and Church House staff.

Texas, Maurice M. Benitez, Bishop.

Friday: West Missouri, John Clark Buchanan, Bishop. PRAISE GOD for the growth in the diocese; and for two new churches which were planted two years ago and have taken root as viable congregations. PRAY for the start of a third new congregation this year and for continued renewal in established parishes and missions.

West Texas, John H. MacNaughton, Bishop. PRAY for the diocese as it elects a Bishop Coadjutor and as it continues its vision in a major advance fund and ministry program to be executed over the next three years.

Saturday: Western Kansas, John F. Ashby, Bishop.
Western Louisiana, Robert J. Hargrove, Jr., Bishop.

> *God our Father*
> *in Christ you make all things new:*
> *transform the poverty of our nature*
> *by the riches of your grace*
> *and reveal your glory*
> *in the renewal of our lives;*
> *through Jesus Christ our Lord.*
> (A South African Prayer)

PRAY for the Anglican Church of Papua New Guinea, Bevan Meredith, Archbishop, with its five dioceses.

Papua New Guinea is a nation under stress. Predominantly a nation of subsistence agriculture with strong village traditions accentuated by fierce topography, it is also rich in natural resources which offer a prosperous place in the world economy (with which it has had, in historical terms, only brief contact). A result is a clash of cultures and values which any young nation would find difficult to resolve.

The "mainline" churches are an important factor in the future. Teaching and showing the love of Christ for all God's children and serving them with educational and medical services, our mission to preach the gospel brings a new knowledge of God's grace to individual souls. At the same time it implants values which Papua New Guineans need in the difficult business of building a modern nation without throwing away the better parts of our traditional cultures.

PRAY that the Anglican Church of Papua New Guinea will uphold the unity and love of Christians one for another in a nation still marred by tribal enmities and violence, and will care for those for whom life is hard, especially in the major towns and cities.

Monday: Aipo Rongo, Paul Richardson, Bishop. PRAY for work in translating the liturgy and the scriptures into the many local languages of the diocese and for the inculturation of worship and theology. GIVE THANKS for Kerina College and its work of training catechists and for the ministry of catechists in the diocese.

Tuesday: Dogura, Tevita Afu Talanoa, Bishop. GIVE THANKS for the assistance through the Centenary and the Dogura Trade Store in purchasing a diocesan boat. PRAY for the development of our Team Ministry and for more participation by the laity in the life of the church; for our new Bishop and the synod to be held this year; and for isolated parishes and lonely priests, that they may experience the fellowship of the Holy Spirit.

Wednesday: New Guinea Islands, Archbishop Bevan Meredith, Bishop. GIVE THANKS for the ordination of the new Bishop of Dogura, formerly provost of the New Guinea Island Cathedral Church, Rabaul. PRAY for newly ordained deacons and priests, that they may be faithful to their calling; and for an increase in vocations to the sacred ministry; and for peace and justice throughout the world, especially for the peoples of Bougainville Island.

Thursday: Popondota, Walter Siba, Bishop. PRAY for the ministry of the Popondetta Christian Community Centre to unemployed youth in the town area, and for mutual understanding between the people of Oro Province and temporary residents from other provinces and countries. GIVE THANKS for the establishment of two new parishes, and for the restraining influence of Christian priests and lay people in potentially violent situations.

Friday: Port Moresby, Isaac Gadebo, Bishop.

Saturday: PRAY for teachers in church schools.

Father in heaven, we give thanks for life, and the experiences life brings us. We thank you for our joys, sorrows, trials, failures and triumphs. Above all we thank you for the hope we have in Christ that we shall find fulfillment in him. We praise you for our country, its beauty, the riches it has for us and the gifts it showers on us. We thank you for your peoples, the gift of languages we speak, the variety of races we have, the cultural heritage we cherish and the latent possibilities there are for our country to be great. Grant that we accept these gifts with thankfulness and use them for the good of the human race and to bring glory to you.

(*Arati,* Calcutta Diocesan Newsletter)

Province of Papua New Guinea

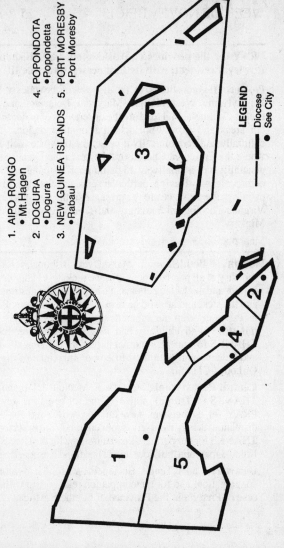

1. AIPO RONGO
   • Mt. Hagen

2. DOGURA
   • Dogura

3. NEW GUINEA ISLANDS
   • Rabaul

4. POPONDOTA
   • Popondetta

5. PORT MORESBY
   • Port Moresby

LEGEND
—— Diocese
• See City

PRAY for the province of Washington, USA, Bishop Robert Rowley, President, with its 13 dioceses. (province III)

Province III is constituted by the dioceses of the states of Virginia, Pennsylvania, West Virginia, Maryland, Delaware, and the District of Columbia. Included are the differences of major metropolitan areas and rural Appalachian Mountain regions. Racially, culturally and economically diverse, the province includes areas where the Episcopal Church first began in the United States and generally has a relatively high number of congregations and communicants. Having particular influence on the life of the people in the province are the presence of the nation's capital, the Virginia Theological Seminary and Trinity Episcopal School for Ministry.

Map, pp. 22-23.

Monday: **Bethlehem,** J. Mark Dyer, Bishop. PRAY for the ministry of all baptized people as we seek to see and serve Christ in poor and neglected persons: the homeless, the destitute, the old and the sick, and all who have none to care for them. PRAY for us as we develop our ministries of advocacy and justice, new ministries with children, and new faith communities. GIVE THANKS for our new partnerships with the Diocese of Meath and Kildare, and with the Moscow Patriarchate of the Russian Orthodox Church.

Central Pennsylvania, Charlie F. McNutt, Jr., Bishop. GIVE THANKS for faithful ministries and for generous stewardship. PRAY for evangelism, new mission work; and for efforts to dismantle racism in ourselves, our churches and in society. GIVE THANKS for our partnership in mission with the Diocese of Kita Kanto, Japan, and the Dioceses of Dhaka and Kushtia, Bangladesh.

Delaware, Cabell Tennis, Bishop. PRAY for the mission of each congregation; and for the companion relationship with the Diocese of Pretoria in the Province of Southern Africa.

Tuesday: Easton, Martin Townsend, Bishop. PRAY for the continuing education of the clergy and for the re-inspiration of some struggling congregations.

Maryland, Charles L. Longest, Bishop-in-Charge. GIVE THANKS for God's blessings during the episcopate of A. Theodore Eastman, who retired early this year. PRAY for the diocese throughout an interim period of self-study in preparation for the election of a new diocesan bishop.

Wednesday: Northwestern Pennsylvania, Robert D. Rowley, Jr., Bishop. GIVE THANKS for the ministries of laity and clergy; and for new ministry opportunities. PRAY for our renewal in Christ Jesus and our growing unity through him.

Pennsylvania, Allen L. Bartlett, Jr., Bishop; Franklin Turner, Suffragan. GIVE THANKS for our Baptismal Covenant. PRAY that we may be empowered and equipped for the proclamation of the gospel and social ministry in metropolitan Philadelphia; and for the planting of new, and redevelopment of old, congregations.

Thursday: Pittsburgh, Alden M. Hathaway, Bishop. PRAY for the planting of new churches; for our Long Range Planning process, redesigning our organization and priorities as a diocese for development, outreach and evangelism; for our work with other communions in developing an aggressive urban mission toward a spiritual renaissance in the City of Pittsburgh. GIVE THANKS for our rich and challenging diversity and opportunity to bear witness to Jesus Christ in the steel valley.

Southern Virginia, Frank Harris Vest, Jr., Bishop. PRAY for our efforts to address institutional racism, to prepare for the creation of two new dioceses out of the present one, to work among the poor and oppressed, and to become evangelists for Christ.

Friday: Southwestern Virginia, A. Heath Light, Bishop. PRAY for the 75th anniversary celebration of the establishment of the diocese, which coincides with the 75th anniversary of the establishment of our companion diocese of Bradford in England. There is anticipation of a shared celebration. PRAY also for the Rev. Dr. Edwin Pearse, Deputy for Congregational and Clergy Development. GIVE THANKS for the reconciliation of the church in the Sudan, another companion in mission, and PRAY for political peace in the Sudan.

Virginia, Peter James Lee, Bishop. PRAY for evangelism and new churches; for congregational development in existing churches; for outreach to human need; for mutual ministries with overseas dioceses; and for two new suffragan bishops.

Saturday: Washington (USA), Ronald H. Haines, Bishop; Jane H. Dixon, Suffragan. PRAY that we be more effective in proclaiming the gospel in a multi-cultural, multi-racial society; that we be able to increase our outreach to the poor; and that we discern God's will as we plan for the future.

West Virginia (USA), John H. Smith, Bishop. GIVE THANKS for the ministry of the laity, which is having an increasing impact on the life and mission of the diocese; for the ministry of evangelism and the success of the Capital Funds Drive which has enabled new vision for mission. PRAY for the Jubilee Centers of ministry and for the ministry of the diocese among the peoples of Appalachia, where issues of poverty and of economic justice are essential.

Lord of lords, Creator of all things,
God of all things, God over all gods,
God of sun and rain, you created the earth with a thought
and us with your breath.

Lord, we brought in the harvest.
The rain watered the earth,
the sun drew cassava and corn out of the clay.
Your mercy showered blessing after blessing over our lands.

Creeks grew into rivers: swamps became lakes.
Healthy fat cows graze on the green sea of the savanna.
The rain smoothed out the clay walls:
the mosquitoes perished in the high waters.

Lord, the yam is fat like meat, the cassava melts on the tongue,
oranges burst in their peels, dazzling and bright.
Lord, nature gives thanks, your creatures give thanks.
Your praise rises in us like the great river.
Lord of lords, Creator, Provider,
we thank you in the name of Jesus Christ.

(West Africa)

PRAY for the Church of the Province of Myanmar (Burma— Myanmanainggan Karityan Athindaw), Andrew U. Mya Han, Archbishop, with its six dioceses.

Although a democratic government was elected early in 1990, the Burmese military regime has refused to yield up its power. Opposition leaders, including Aung San Suu Kyi, have been held in detention, and torture, victimisation and political exile have all remained realities. A United Nations commission visiting the country in 1991 commented on its lack of access to notable leaders. Over 15,000 people have fled the country to avoid arrest. At least 3,000 more are held in appalling conditions. The report advocated strong international pressure on the regime to give way to democracy.

PRAY for all those working for democracy; for the military regime, that light will dawn; for those able to exercise political and economic pressure; and for the churches in all their struggles for reconciliation and liberation.

Monday: Pa'an, Daniel Hoi Kyin, Bishop.

Tuesday: Mandalay, Andrew Hla Aung, Bishop. PRAY for the extension of the Christian centre and for the training of the third batch of catechists; and for work in the mission areas of Tamu, Naga Hills and Southern Shan State.

(St. Cecilia's Day) **PRAY for church musicians.**

Wednesday: Myitkyina, Timothy Mya Wah, Archbishop Commissionary. GIVE THANKS for the renovation and extension of the Cathedral completed recently. PRAY for plans to fully organise the diocese. GIVE THANKS for encouragement in mission areas.

Thursday *(Thanksgiving Day, USA)*—**Sittwe,** Barnabas Htaung Hawi, Bishop. PRAY for the tithing programme which is encouraging and gradually being accepted; for the diocese to consolidate the family spirit; and for more people to come forward for full-time ministry.

Friday: Toungoo, George Kyaw Mya, Bishop. GIVE THANKS for this newly formed diocese; for new church buildings in Loikaw, Kayah State, and in Toungoo. PRAY for the new Bishop; for the evangelism programmes among ethnic groups; for displaced families in distress; for peace and tranquility in the country; and for Bishop George Kyaw Mya in his retirement.

Saturday: Yangon (Rangoon), Archbishop Andrew Mya Han, Bishop; Assistant Bishop, Samuel San Sihtay. PRAY for plans to renovate and repair Bishop's Home building, which is the office of the diocese, to provide quarters for visiting clergy from the Province and for Christians who come to Yangon for medical treatment; and for evangelism consultant training, training of missionary personnel, expansion of literature programmes, training of village school teachers; and for the clergy seminar and Silver Jubilee of the Province which will be held in 1995.

Province of Myanmar (Burma)

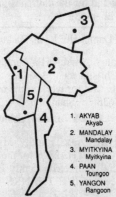

1. AKYAB
   Akyab
2. MANDALAY
   Mandalay
3. MYITKYINA
   Myitkyina
4. PAAN
   Toungoo
5. YANGON
   Rangoon

The Church in Ceylon (Sri Lanka)

1. COLOMBO
   ●Colombo
2. KURUNAGALA
   ●Kurunagala

PRAY for the Philippine Episcopal Church, Narcisco Ticobay, Prime Bishop, with its five dioceses.

In a country that is 89 percent Roman Catholic, there are over 86,000 Anglicans. There are 123 parishes and 140 clergy. St. Andrew's Theological Seminary in Manila is the Province's theological college. The population of the Philippines totals more than 52,000,000.

With its history as a Spanish colony in the 16th century the Philippines became a predominantly Roman Catholic country. However, in 1898, when the Americans colonised the area, Bishop Charles Henry Brent of the USA established missionary work in Northern Luzon and among the Muslim populations in the South. In 1990 the Philippine Episcopal Church became an autonomous Province of the Anglican Communion. The first Philippine bishop was E.G. Longid, consecrated in 1963.

Monday: **Central Philippines,** Manuel C. Lumpias, Bishop.

Tuesday: **North Central Philippines,** Joel A. Pachao, Bishop.

Wednesday *(St. Andrew)*—**PRAY for His All-Holiness the Ecumenical Patriarch of Constantinople.**

Northern Luzon, Ignacio C. Soliba, Bishop.

Thursday: **Northern Philippines,** Robert O. Longid, Bishop. PRAY for the peace process/talks addressing root causes of conflict; for making conflict more humane; for tribal and community-based programs; for mission consciousness and engagement; for reversal of bio-social degradation; for total ministry training; for production/distribution of indigenous scripture editions; for calamity damage rehabilitation; and for resources development.

Friday: **Southern Philippines,** Narcisco V. Ticobay, Prime Bishop.

Saturday: **PRAY for the Philippine Independent Church, Tito Pasco, Supreme Bishop.**

Philippine Episcopal Church

1. CENTRAL
   PHILIPPINES
   ●Quezon City
2. NORTHERN LUZON
   ●Bulanao
3. NORTHERN PHILIPPINES
   ●Boutoc
4. SOUTHERN PHILIPPINES
   ●Cotabato City
5. NORTH-CENTRAL
   PHILIPPINES
   ●

PRAY for the province of Queensland, Australia, Peter J. Hollingworth, Archbishop, with its five dioceses.

The province consists of the State of Queensland and the Northern Territory and is a large rural area, rich in natural resources, yet facing significant problems and challenges for ministry.

Three major issues confront us at present. The first is the acute crisis facing the rural sector involving the worst drought in 50 years, coupled with a rural recession caused by the domestic drop in world commodity prices and the loss of traditional export markets. This has led to the slaughtering of livestock and the stockpiling of wool and wheat when much of the world is hungry. The rural crisis has had a direct impact on many of our rural churches, both through the loss of regular income and an increase in welfare aid disbursements. Many families may have to walk off their properties if effective long-term rural restructuring cannot be achieved and short term financial relief provided by government.

The second, by way of contrast, is the rapid urban growth occurring in South East Queensland, which is the fastest growing area in Australia. Growing numbers of people have become part of a vast urban agglomeration lacking much sense of community and without adequate support services. The church has very limited prospects in establishing traditional parishes and will need to find alternative ways of establishing local congregations as springboards of mission and ministry.

The third issue concerns the situation of aboriginal and islander people who seek justice and human dignity, especially in this United Nations Year for the Indigenous Peoples of the World. They seek land rights and powers of self-determination, particularly in the wake of a recent High Court determination in principle in their favour. Their empowerment will help both to maintain traditional lifestyles and practices as well as taking their full place in the wider society.

PRAY that Almighty God will look mercifully upon all his people, that his justice will be manifested, and that they, being supported by communities of faith, may find in his Son Jesus Christ the fulfillment of their hopes as children made in God's image.

Map, p. 28.

Monday: Brisbane, Archbishop Peter Hollingworth and Regional Bishops Clyde Wood, John Noble and Ron Williams. PRAY for the diocese as it considers a new pastoral strategy based upon three new regions, in order to meet the demands of the most rapidly growing area in Australia.

Tuesday: Carpentaria, Anthony Hall-Matthews, Bishop. PRAY for the further inculturation of the gospel in Aboriginal and Torres Strait Islander Communities. GIVE THANKS for the discovery that the Catechumenal Process fits in with the pattern of the Aboriginal traditional initiation process and so gives hope for a new break-through in evangelisation.

Wednesday: North Queensland, John Lewis, Bishop; Arthur Malcolm and Ian Stuart, Assistants; George Tung Yep, retired. PRAY for ministries for Aborigines of Palm Island and Yarrabah, and the Torres Strait Island Ministry in Townsville; and for diocesan schools and facilities for the elderly.

Thursday: Northern Territory, Richard Appleby, Bishop. GIVE THANKS for the translation and publication of the scriptures in the Aboriginal languages of the diocese. PRAY for those who work with the Aboriginal parishes in the areas of literacy and substance abuse.

Friday *(Tanzania Day)*—**PRAY for Tanzania.**

Saturday: Rockhampton, George A. Hearn, Bishop. PRAY for the development of the catechumenate and the formation of new Christians in our parishes; for the ministry of rural parishes affected by drought and recession; and for our focus in the Decade of Evangelism in 1994 on ministry with families.

Gracious and holy Father, give us wisdom to perceive you, diligence to seek you, patience to wait for you, eyes to behold you, a heart to meditate on you, and a life to proclaim you; through the power of the Spirit of Jesus Christ our Lord.

(Saint Benedict)

PRAY for the province of Sewanee, USA, Bishop Duncan Gray, President, with its 20 dioceses. (province IV)

The twenty dioceses of province IV stretch from the tip of Florida to the outer banks of North Carolina and from the Mississippi River to the Gulf of Mexico. The symbolic center for the province is at Sewanee, Tennessee, where The University of the South stands. Each diocese is an "owning diocese" of the educational institution which includes St. Luke's Seminary. Kanuga Conference Center is also a center for meetings and conferences, especially for the youth of the province. The province budgets for a youth coordinator as well as a coordinator for ministry to higher education.

Ministry with an already large and growing Hispanic population has been going on for some time in Florida and in the dioceses where Spanish-speaking people live. We ask your prayers for that work, especially with the farm workers, both migrant and permanent. There is an on-going ministry with Haitians and several dioceses have companion relationships with Haiti.

Finally, the province has, along with the national church, been involved with a discussion of human sexuality. Nearly every diocese took part in that study in a formal way and, hopefully, those discussions and study and dialogue will continue beyond the 1994 General Convention.

PRAY for these ministries and keep them in your thoughts and prayers.

Map, pp. 22-23.

Monday *(Kenya Day)*—PRAY for Kenya.

Alabama, Robert Oran Miller, Bishop. GIVE THANKS for the expansion of ministry to higher education. PRAY for our initiative in lay ministry.

Atlanta, Frank Kellogg Allan, Bishop.

Central Florida, John W. Howe, Bishop; Reginald Hollis, and Herbert Edmondson, Assistants. GIVE THANKS for the restructuring of the diocese to promote new mission and ministry at the local level. PRAY for the six new congregations started already and for the nine more planned by the end of the Decade of Evangelism.

Tuesday: Central Gulf Coast, Charles F. Duvall, Bishop. GIVE THANKS for dedicated clergy and committed laity who have started five new congregations in the '80s and one so far in the '90s. PRAY for continued exploration of ways to share the gospel with the unchurched through "HELLO" Ministries and other programs.

East Carolina, Brice Sidney Sanders, Bishop.

East Tennessee, Robert Gould Tharp, Bishop. PRAY that the diocese will respond to the call for evangelism and in thanksgiving for newly established missions.

Florida, Robert P. Varley, Bishop in Residence.

Wednesday: Georgia, Harry W. Shipps, Bishop. PRAY for Belize, our companion diocese, and our joint programs; for our ministry among African-Americans; for our vocational diaconal ministries, especially to those with AIDS; and for our ministry in small towns.

Kentucky, Bishop to be chosen. With the ordination of the VIIth Bishop of Kentucky in 1994, the diocese will undergo transition, change and challenge. PRAY for the new Bishop and for those who work with the Bishop; for small churches and their area ministers; for churches in the metropolitan areas of the diocese; for the founding of a new congregation in 1994; and for the survival of several marginal churches. GIVE THANKS for 162 years of growth under the first six bishops.

Lexington, Don A. Wimberly, Bishop. PRAY for our new missions being planned and started in the central and northern regions of Kentucky.

Thursday: Louisiana, James B. Brown, Bishop. PRAY for an increase of evangelism in the parishes and spiritual growth in the clergy.

Mississippi, Alfred C. Marble, Jr., Bishop. PRAY for the diocese as it seeks to strengthen its mission and ministry with a new staff and reorganized structure.

North Carolina, Bishop to be chosen; Huntington Williams, Jr. Suffragan. PRAY for our diocese and its new bishop; for the long-range planning process; and for our continuing work in areas of social ministry, higher education, and overseas relationships.

South Carolina, Edward Salmon, Jr., Bishop. PRAY for the bishops, clergy and people; for congregational development; for leadership training; and for our companion relationship with Northern Argentina.

Friday: **Southeast Florida,** Calvin O. Schofield, Jr., Bishop. PRAY for continued rebuilding from Hurricane Andrew; for spiritual reawakening throughout the diocese; for the establishing of new congregations; and for the revitalization of many of our existing parishes.

Southwest Florida, Rogers S. Harris, Bishop; Telesforo A. Isaac, Assistant. PRAY for our youth and third-age evangelism, Hispanic ministry, and pastoral outreach to the lapsed. GIVE THANKS for growth, for the catechumenate, for DaySpring Conference Center, and for ecumenical bridges built in Pontifax.

Tennessee, Bertram N. Herlong, Bishop-elect. PRAY for our mission, to release, empower, and equip the people of God to minister in restoring all persons to unity with God and one another in Christ. GIVE THANKS that the Holy Spirit is moving the church to a new understanding of ministry by all the baptized, a servanthood by persons to persons after the manner of Jesus Christ.

Saturday: **Upper South Carolina,** William A. Beckham, Bishop; William F. Carr, Assistant. PRAY for ministries to youth and the aging; for our continuing work in Haiti; for our work in evangelism with the aging and those suffering from Alzheimer's; and for better stewardship of our environment.

West Tennessee, Alex D. Dickson, Bishop. PRAY that we may discern God's will in the election of a Bishop Coadjutor; and for growth in Cell Group Evangelism.

Western North Carolina, Robert H. Johnson, Bishop. PRAY for our Centennial Witness Fund Drive to undergird our Human Hurt and Hope outreach effort, to establish new congregations, and to restore the fabric of parishes and institutions. PRAY for God's guidance in the establishment of a cathedral and for continued increasing involvement of both laity and clergy in proclaiming the love of Christ.

PRAY for the Church of Nigeria, Joseph A. Adetiloye, Archbishop, with its 41 dioceses.

In a vast geographical area of 923,768 square miles, Nigeria, one of the fastest growing Provinces of the Anglican Communion, has a total population of 120,000,000. The Provincial Office is in Lagos. Over 40 percent of the population of Nigeria is Christian, with 40 percent being Muslim.

A rebirth of Christianity began with the arrival of Christian freed slaves in Nigeria in the middle of the 19th century. The Church Missionary Society responded to this situation by establishing churches, schools and an evangelistic ministry throughout the country, particularly in the south. In often difficult circumstances, the church maintains a strong witness to Christ and began the Decade of Evangelism by consecrating nine Missionary Bishops for work in Northern Nigeria. These Bishops will reach out into areas that have hitherto been untouched by Christianity.

Monday: Aba, A.O. Iwuagwu, Bishop. PRAY for on-going renewal, evangelism and church growth, that all may move in the right direction; for clergy education; for the alleviation of poverty and misery among the rural communities; for our links with Churches in England and in ECUSA.

Abuja, Peter Jasper Akinola, Bishop. GIVE THANKS for signs of growth in mission and for growing commitment and ministry of our laity. PRAY for our rural development programmes and for continuing relevance of the church to the larger society.

Akoko, Jacob O.K. Olowokure, Bishop.

Akure, Emmanuel B. Gbonigi, Bishop. THANK GOD for inspiring celebrations of our tenth anniversary. PRAY for God's blessing on the links between Liverpool and Akure and South Rwenzori in Uganda and Akure; and for a government of righteousness, probity, public accountability, justice, peace and prosperity.

Tuesday: Asaba, R.N.C. Nwosu, Bishop. THANK GOD for the decision of our diocese to complete her new All Saints' Cathedral before the end of this Decade of Evangelism. PRAY that the

Almighty God will inspire and strengthen all the clergy and the laity to achieve this great goal.

Awka, Maxwell S.C. Anikwenwa, Bishop. THANK GOD for his love and care; for understanding among the clergy and laity. PRAY for St. Paul's University College, Awka; St. Mary the Virgin Convent, Ufuma; Bishop Crowther Junior Seminary; Projects in the Village of Faith; and for challenging ministry in the new Capital Territory, Awka.

Bauchi, E.O. Chukwuma, Bishop. Pray for peaceful co-existence between Christians and Muslims in this part of the country, and for God's strengthening power in the faith of the people.

Benin, John K. George, Bishop.

Wednesday *(St. Thomas)*—**PRAY for the Mar Thoma Syrian Church of Malabar (India),** Alexander Mar Thoma, Metropolitan.

Calabar, Wilfried G. Ekprikpo, Bishop.

Egba, Titus Ilori Akintayo, Bishop. THANK GOD for the fulfilment of his promise, "I am with you always"; may this continue to be true of Nigeria and all nations.

Egbado, T.I.O. Bolaji, Bishop. THANK GOD for the successful implementation of the programmes of the Diocesan Board of Evangelism. PRAY for the new Diocesan Board of Education, that its impact may be felt on both Sunday school and children's service; and that women's works and the Women Awareness Sunday may achieve the desired results.

Ekiti, Clement A. Akinbola, Bishop.

Thursday: Enugu, Gideon N. Otubelu, Bishop. GIVE THANKS for God's blessings in the first 25 years of our diocese. PRAY for spiritual growth of newly established congregations; and for the nation and in the struggle to solve our economic and political problems.

Ibadan, Gideon N. Olajide, Bishop.

Ife, G.B. Oloniyo, Bishop. PRAY for the continual interest of the laity in the work of the diocese.

Ijebu (Nigeria), Abraham O. Olowoyo, Bishop.

Friday: Ijebu-Remo, Elijah O.I. Ogundana, Bishop. THANK GOD for the successful celebrations of our tenth anniversary. PRAY for a new vision for the spiritual and physical growth of the diocese.

Ilesa, Ephraim A. Ademowo, Bishop. THANK GOD for his sustaining grace in these trying times in our nation; for improvements on the basics of our faith—intensive Bible study, prayer and sacraments. PRAY for clergy and laity; for youth, women's work, new churches, city-wide crusades and the diocesan School of Theology and Church Music.

Jos, Benjamin A. Kwashi, Bishop. THANK GOD for new churches; for the opening of the Christian Institute; and for the acquisition of land. PRAY that God will direct these developments and that both clergy and laity will commit themselves to Christ and to the work of the Holy Spirit.

Kaduna, Titus E. Ogbonyomi, Bishop. PRAY for those whose Christian lives and witnesses are being tried, that God may continue to uphold them in their bid to reach the unreached; and that the plan to return the nation to a democratically elected government may be peaceful.

Saturday: Kafanchan, William Weh Diya, Bishop.

Kano, Benjamin O. Omosebi, Bishop. PRAY for the increase of God-chosen people to serve in the vast, untended areas of the diocese; and for the financial resources to meet their training and salaries.

Katsina, James Shekari Kwasu, Bishop.

O God, our heavenly Father, we bow in wonder at your gift to us at Christmas, far surpassing any gift that we can ever offer. Let us not forget those who have no gift but yours, although they may not know it. Give us your compassion, that we may seek and find them, and give them what you have given us, the abundant life and humble love of him who made Christmas mean what it is, your Son our Savior Jesus Christ.

(Massey H. Shepherd, Jr.)

Province of Nigeria

DIOCESAN CENTRES

1.	Lagos	21.	Aba
2.	Ijebu	22.	Niger Delta
3.	Ijebu-Remo	23.	Kwara
4.	Egba Egbado	24.	Abuja
5.	Ibadan	25.	Jos
6.	Osun	26.	Kaduna
7.	Ilesha	27.	Kano
8.	Ondo	28.	Makurdi
9.	Owo	29.	Yola
10.	Akure	30.	Minna
11.	Ekiti	31.	Katanchan
12.	Akoko	32.	Sokoto
13.	Benin	33.	Katsina
14.	Warri	34.	Bauchi
15.	Asaba	35.	Maiduguri
16.	The Niger	36.	Egbado
17.	Awka	37.	Ife
18.	Enugu	38.	Uyo
19.	Owerri	39.	Calabar
20.	Okigwe-Orlu		

LEGEND

— Province

--- State Boundries

• See City

Lift up your hearts in prayer. Lift up your voices in praise. Let your eyes rise in expectation, and your hands in exultation, for the Lord has drawn near, and dwells among us.

Monday *(St. Stephen)*—**PRAY for Christians under persecution.**

Kwara (Nigeria), Herbert Hanine, Bishop. PRAY for the Lord's blessings on our renewed sense of commitment to evangelism and especially for the new churches that are being planted; and for more resources to complete the Mothers' Union and the W.G. Project for young women.

Lagos (Nigeria), Archbishop Joseph A. Adetiloye, Bishop.

Madugur (Nigeria), Emmanuel K. Mani, Bishop.

Tuesday *(St. John)*—**PRAY for refugees and those who minister to them.**

Makurdi (Nigeria), N.N. Inyom, Bishop. PRAY for our four development programs: evangelism and church planting, our Rural Health Program, education in-service training, and Agriculture and Rural Development. PRAY for continued commitment and devotion on the part of the clergy and laity to evangelism.

Mbaise (Nigeria), Cyril Chukwa Nanyanwu, Bishop.

Minna (Nigeria), Nathaniel Yisa, Bishop. GIVE THANKS for consecration of the new bishop; and for opportunity for evangelism and steady growth. PRAY for wisdom, courage and fortitude as we move forward in the power of the Holy Spirit with manpower and other resource development in the face of runaway economic crisis, political and social uncertainty.

The Niger (Nigeria), Jonathan Arinzechukwu Onyemelukwe, Bishop.

Wednesday *(Holy Innocents)*—**PRAY for all children.**

The Niger Delta (Nigeria), Samuel O. Elenwa, Bishop.

Oke Osun (Nigeria), Abraham Oluyemi Awosan, Bishop. THANK GOD for the successful inauguration of the diocese on

St. Paul's Day, January 25, 1993; for the consuming zeal for evangelism and youth work already in existence. PRAY that God may supply all our needs in terms of personnel, finance and spiritual growth; and for a peaceful, prosperous and God-fearing civilian government.

Okigwe-Orlu (Nigeria), Samuel C.N. Ebo, Bishop. THANK GOD for a strong sense of evangelism pervading the entire diocese. PRAY that Christians may stand firm in their faith amidst a present flood of false doctrines and commercialised religions; that the envisaged subdivision of the diocese may be guided by the Holy Spirit; and that the ship of our nation tossed to and fro may finally arrive safely at the haven of its journey.

Thursday: Ondo (Nigeria), Samuel O. Aderin, Bishop.

Osun (Nigeria), Seth O. Fabbemi, Bishop. PRAY for the planting of new churches; for our mission of evangelism and outreach; for the work of the Mothers' Union in the rural areas and among new converts; for the Diocesan Advisor on Mission and Evangelism; for the Mothers' Union worker; and for funds to purchase a van and equipment for the work of evangelism.

Owerri (Nigeria), Benjamin C. Nwankiti, Bishop. PRAY that, led by the Spirit, the people may powerfully proclaim the gospel; and that the church in Owerri may grow by house to house evangelism. THANK GOD for the witness of youths and the women in leading persons to Christ.

Friday: Owo (Nigeria), Peter A. Adebiyi, Bishop.

Sokoto (Nigeria), Josiah Idowu-Fearon, Bishop.

Uyo (Nigeria), Ebenezar E. Nglass, Bishop.

Saturday: Warri (Nigeria), Nathaniel A. Enuku, Bishop. THANK GOD for the evangelistic zeal in the diocese. PRAY for a true spirit of reconciliation and forgiveness in the diocese.

Yola (Nigeria), Christian O. Efobi, Bishop. GIVE THANKS for the completion of the permanent Bishop's Court and effective mission within the diocese. PRAY for our spiritual growth, sense of unity and commitment of the clergy and the laity; and for greater identification of our basic needs.

PATTERNS OF ANGLICAN PARTNERSHIP

The Anglican Communion, which exists on all continents, is a fellowship—within the One, Holy, Catholic, and Apostolic Church—of churches in communion with each other and with the See of Canterbury. The relationship among them is based on a common history, deriving from the Church of England, a common tradition of doctrine, discipline and worship, and mutual responsibility and interdependence in their mission. It is a freely chosen partnership, with emphasis on autonomy and independence. The Archbishop of Canterbury, honored as "first among equals," is a symbol of unity among 70 million Anglicans, and frequently serves as their spokesman in international and ecumenical affairs. Other symbols of unity are *The Book of Common Prayer*—in many different versions and translations—and the Lambeth Conference, which brings together all diocesan bishops for consultations once a decade. English language and culture, formerly important bonds of unity, are now less significant as the Anglican Communion grows rapidly in Africa, Asia and other non-English-speaking regions.

A Diocese is an aggregation of parishes and mission congregations under the administrative and pastoral care of a bishop. In Anglican tradition a "local church" consists of all who share the leadership of the same bishop. A goal of Anglican mission is to establish an independent church in each country where Anglicans are found in sufficient numbers to make this possible.

Provinces: There are many Provinces in the Anglican Communion, each one indicating a national church or geographical area incorporating a number of dioceses. They are usually under the leadership of an Archbishop or a Presiding Bishop. There are two kinds of provinces: one, an autonomous church in the Anglican Communion, usually spelled with a capital P, as the Province of Melanesia; and two, a regional cluster of dioceses within a large national church, an internal province, usually spelled with a small p, as in Canada or USA.

Lambeth: As Anglicanism spread during the 19th century, it was felt desirable that all diocesan bishops should meet together from time to time, to coordinate planning, strengthen the bonds of unity, and to consult about major issues. The first Lambeth Conference was held in 1867 at Lambeth Palace, the residence of the Archbishop of Canterbury. The next conference will be held in 1998.

The Anglican Consultative Council (ACC), with a permanent staff headed by a Secretary General, meets once every two or three years and consists of one, two or three members selected by each member Province. It includes bishops, priests and lay men and women who have experience of what the church has to grapple with in their own part of the world. The Archbishop of Canterbury is the president of the council and is chairman of the first session of each meeting. The chairman of ACC is the Rev. Canon Colin Craston.

The Primates Meeting: In addition, the Primates or heads of the member-churches of the Anglican Communion have begun to meet every two or three years. The Primates assist in developing the agenda for meetings of the Anglican Consultative Council and the Lambeth Conference and plan for the implementation of their recommendations.

The Theological and Doctrinal Consultation: This is a new instrument of international consultation and cooperation among Anglicans. The first was composed of fourteen distinguished theologians, some of them lay persons, and met three times between 1981 and 1985. In 1986 they published their report, *For the Sake of the Kingdom—God's Church and the New Creation*, which was a preparatory document for the Lambeth Conference 1988.

Inter-Anglican Networks: Composed of Provincial specialists in a number of fields, these networks have been sponsored and assisted (but not funded) by the ACC. These include networks on Youth, Ecumenical Relations, Liturgy, Peace and Justice issues, the Anglican Publishers Consortium, and the Mission Issues and Strategy Advisory Group (MISAG). The last has published a parish study guide based on stories from many parts of the world, *Renew Our Vision in Evangelism*, available from Forward Movement Publications (US $3.75, postpaid.).

For more information about, and maps of, the Anglican Communion, see *Who Are the Anglicans*, 1988, Forward Movement Publications, US $3.50, postpaid, and *The Anglican Communion, a guide*, 1991, Church House Publishing, London, £2.95.

ADDRESSES

Anglican Consultative Council, Partnership House, 157 Waterloo Rd., London SE18UT England

Aotearo, New Zealand and Polynesia, P.O. Box 2148, Rotorua, New Zealand

Australia, P.O. Box Q190, Queen Victoria P.O., Sydney 2000, NSW, Australia

Bangladesh, 54 Johnson Rd., Dhaka 1, Bangladesh

Brazil, Caixa Postal 965, 91700 P. Alegre, RS Brazil

Burundi, BP 1300 Buja, Bujumbura, Burundi

Canada, 600 Jarvis St., Toronto, Ontario M4Y 2J6 Canada

Central Africa, P.O. Box 769, Gaborone, Botswana

East Asia, P.O. Box 811, Koto Kinabalu, Sabah, Malaysia

England, Church House, Dean's Yard, London SW1P 3NZ England

Indian Ocean, Box 44, Mahe, Seychelles

Ireland, Church of Ireland House, Church Avenue, Rathmines, Dublin 6, Ireland

Japan, 65-3 Yarai-cho Shinjuku-ku, Tokyo 161, Japan

Jerusalem and Middle East, P.O. Box 2075, Nicosia 118, Cyprus

Kenya, P.O. Box 40502, Nairobi, Kenya

Korea, 3 Chong Dong, Chung Ku, Seoul, 100-120, Korea

Melanesia, P.O. Box 19, Honiara, Solomon Islands

Myanmar (Burma), 140 Pyidaungsu-Yeiktha Rd. Dagon P.O. 1191, Yangon (Rangoon), Myanmar

Nigeria, P.O. Box 78, Lagos, Nigeria

North India, Bishop's House, Darjeeling 734101 W Bengal, India

Pakistan, Bishop's House, P.O. Box 27, Mission Rd., Gojra Faisallabad, Pakistan

Papua New Guinea, Box 304, Lae, M.P., Papua New Guinea

Philippines, P.O. Box 3167, Manila

Rwanda, BP 15, Vunga, Via Ruhengeli, Rwanda

Scotland, 121 Grosvenor Cres., Edinburgh EH12 5EE, Scotland

Southern Africa, P.O. Box 61394, Marshalltown, 2107, RSA

Southern Cone, Casilla 50675, Santiago, Chile

South India, Bishop's House Cathedral Compound Medak 502110 Andhra Pradesh, India

Sri Lanka (Ceylon), 368/1 Bauddlaloka Mawatha, Colombo 7, Sri Lanka

Sudan, The Rev. Canon John Kanyikwa, c/o P.O. Box 44838, Nairobi, Kenya

Tanzania, P.O. Box 899, Dodoma, Tanzania

Uganda, P.O. Box 14123, Kampala, Uganda

USA, 815 Second Ave., New York, NY 10017, USA

Wales, 39 Cathedral Rd., S. Glamorgan CF1 9XF, Wales

West Africa, P.O. Box 8, Accra, Ghana

West Indies, Mandeville House, Henry Lane, Collymore Rock, St. Michael, Barbados, West Indies

Zaire, c/o PO21285, Nairobi, Kenya (BP 798, Bunia, Republique du Zaire)

Many prayers in this edition are from *With All God's People, The New Ecumenical Prayer Cycle* published by the World Council of Churches.

INDEX

140

143